2/03   2490

ANN E. WEISS

Adoptions
TODAY
Questions and Controversies

TWENTY-FIRST CENTURY BOOKS
Brookfield, Connecticut

For Malcolm, again,
and with thanks to "Dan"
for sharing his story

Library of Congress Cataloging-in-Publication Data

Weiss, Ann E., 1943-
    Adoptions today : questions and controversies / Ann E. Weiss.
        p. cm.
    Includes bibliographical references and index.
    ISBN 0-7613-1914-X (lib. bdg.)
    1. Adoption—United States—Juvenile literature. [1. Adoption.] I. Title.
HV875.55 .W46 2001 362.73'4—dc21 00-053633

Cover photograph courtesy of © Index Stock Imagery (right) and ©
Jonathan Elderfield / Liaison Agency (left)

Photographs courtesy of © Index Stock Imagery: pp. 2 (Kathy Heister),
122 (Myrleen Cate); Impact Visuals: p. 8 (© Cindy Reiman); The Image
Works Archives: p. 20; Kansas State Historical Society: p. 37; Pam
Hasegawa: p. 56; Liaison Agency: p. 76 (© Jonathan Elderfield); AP/Wide
World Photos: p. 101

Published by Twenty-First Century Books
A Division of The Millbrook Press, Inc.
2 Old New Milford Road, Brookfield, Connecticut 06804
www.millbrookpress.com

CONTENTS

Adoptive parents finalizing an adoption

ADOPTION OVERVIEW 1

Francine Allen was three years old when her mother died in a fire in their Brooklyn, New York, apartment house. Rescued by firefighters, the little girl was rushed to a nearby hospital for emergency treatment. That was on June 2, 1996.

Within weeks, Francine was well enough to be transferred to a rehabilitation center in Manhattan. There she recovered further from her injuries. She made friends with other children at the center. She also began getting regular visits from Michele Sullum, a hospital chaplain and rabbinical student at the Jewish Theological Seminary. Michele had introduced herself to Francine at the request of the child's grandmother, Evelyn Allen.

Evelyn was Francine's only living relative. Evelyn loved her granddaughter, and, like other grandparents, she wanted to stay in touch with the child and watch her grow up. However, since she was legally blind and in poor health, Evelyn could hardly give Francine the kind of home she needed. But who else was there to care for her? (Francine's birth certificate listed her father as "unknown.") It was in order to help solve this dilemma that Evelyn had asked the chaplain to start visiting her grandchild.

Michele sympathized with the grandmother and with Francine. The young chaplain and her husband Jacob, a magazine editor, visited the child frequently, bringing her little presents and playing with her on the grounds of the rehabilitation center. It wasn't long before the couple came to love Francine. In July, less than two months after the fire, Michele suggested to Evelyn that she and Jacob adopt the orphan. Evelyn was delighted and relieved.

A FAMILY FOR FRANCINE

If ever an adoption promised to go smoothly, this one did. Francine needed a home; Michele and Jacob were eager to offer her one. Francine and Evelyn were Jewish; so were the Sullums. Francine had no father, aunts, uncles, or cousins to claim her, and the only relative she did have welcomed the adoption proposal. Surely the adoption would proceed quickly and easily. Michele and Jacob got in touch with the New York City Administration for Children's Services to set the process in motion.

The Sullums soon learned that Francine's adoption, like all formal adoptions in the United States and Canada, would go forward in three distinct steps. First, Evelyn would legally relinquish (give up) her right to raise her granddaughter herself. Next, a judge in Brooklyn's Family Court would place Francine in the temporary custody, or guardianship, of the adoption agency they had chosen to handle her case. At that point, the judge might allow Jacob and Michele to take Francine home to live with them, although she would not yet legally be their daughter. She would become Francine Sullum only when the third and last step was completed—when the judge awarded the Sullums full permanent custody. According to what Jacob and Michele were able to learn from adoption experts, the whole process would take between six months and a year. By mid-1997 at the latest, they reckoned, Francine would have a new birth certificate naming them as her legal parents.

Jacob and Michele were overjoyed at the prospect. Their path to adoption was not an uncommon one; other couples have unexpectedly met or heard about an adoptable child and initiated proceedings. Other couples begin the process by knowing they want a child and actively seeking one out. Many of these couples have chosen adoption after years of trying, and failing, to have biological children of their own. Adoption may have been their only path to the family life they craved. Still others have been touched by news articles about homeless children in the United States or in other countries and have arranged to adopt them.

As it turned out, Francine's adoption did not go as smoothly as the Sullums expected. It took the couple over two months just to get a judge to allow them to move Francine from the rehabilitation center to their home. During that time, Francine—now fully recovered from the effects of the fire—spent most of her waking hours tied into a wheelchair with bedsheets. This confinement was necessary, the rehab staff explained, because older children at the center, some of them severely disabled, might otherwise have run over the three year old with their own wheelchairs. It was sad to see spirited, inquisitive Francine imprisoned in that way, Jacob says. Still, by the end of September, he and Michele had finally installed Francine in a newly decorated room of her own in their Manhattan apartment.

Francine settled in happily in her new home, although she continued to speak of her birth mother from time to time. The Sullums regarded Francine as their own. Yet it would take another agonizing *twenty-six months* before the adoption became final.

Why did it take so long? Jacob Sullum still cannot fully answer that question. Much of what the Sullums went through is routine in adoption cases. Social workers and others repeatedly visited the Sullums' apartment, inspecting it for cleanliness and questioning the couple in depth about their past and present lives, their finances, their child-rearing philosophy, and so on. The Sullums were fingerprinted and required to undergo a criminal background check and to authorize their doctors to fill out detailed health forms. Jacob and Michele also had to provide legal documents to prove beyond any shadow of a doubt that they were in fact married. They were asked to supply home addresses dating back to 1973, when he was eight years old and she only five. They had to work out a schedule of visits between Francine and her grandmother.

Adding to the complications were all the lawyers involved—the Sullums' lawyer, Evelyn's lawyer, Francine's court-appointed attorney. Just managing to get everyone to show up for court hearings at the same date and time could be difficult.

"Now that Francine has been living with us for three years," Jacob wrote in 1999, "there's no question that being her parents was worth all the trouble." But he wonders, "if we had known in advance how emotionally grueling the adoption process would be," whether they would have had the courage to have started it.[1]

Exasperated as Jacob may have been with the adoption process as he experienced it, he understands the purpose behind it. The background checks, lawyers, repeated court appearances, and all the rest are aimed at protecting each side in the adoption triad—adoptees, birth parents, and adoptive families. Thorough checks of prospective parents and their homes protect children who are being adopted. The process also serves to assure birth parents who choose adoption—because of an unplanned pregnancy, perhaps, or because they are single, or feel that they are too young or too poor to support a child—that their child will be raised in a secure and loving home. The process can be useful to prospective (or preadoptive) parents, as well. It tests their resolve to adopt and helps to educate them about a child's wants and needs. The elaborate court proceedings and abundance of lawyers and paperwork also provides them with guarantees that the adoption is legal and cannot be overturned.

ADOPTION—YESTERDAY AND TODAY

There are about two million adopted children under the age of eighteen living in the United States today. Each year, about 150,000 more are adopted, usually as infants (defined as children under the age of two). Roughly two thirds of these children are adopted by relatives. The other 50,000 go, like Francine, to people unrelated to them. In Canada, about 15,000 youngsters are adopted annually.[2] In both countries there are also unknown numbers of children who have not been formally adopted but who live for varying amounts of time with a relative or someone else because their parents are unable or unwilling to care for them.

Then there are those children for whom good adoptive homes cannot be found. By and large, these children are past the newborn and toddler stages at which adoption is easiest. Many are "special needs" children who suffer from physical, mental, or emotional disabilities. Some have brothers and sisters who hope to be adopted together. Finding someone to adopt two or three children as a group is naturally harder than finding someone to adopt a single child. Every year about 110,000 such children enter the foster care system.

Being in foster care can be like being in limbo, with no permanent home. While some foster children will be returned to their birth parents, others have been formally relinquished by their parents or other legal guardians. Still others, though not legally relinquished, have been removed from their families because they have been physically abused or mistreated in some other way. Few of these children are likely to be returned to face future abuse. Most will be sent to live with a foster family on a temporary basis. Some will find adoptive homes. But many others will stay in foster care for years—even most of their childhood. And many of these foster children will be moved from one foster family to another, staying only a few weeks or months in any one home.

Since 1997 the U.S. government has increased its efforts to move foster children into permanent homes. In 1998, 36,000 foster children were adopted in the United States, compared with just 28,000 two years earlier.[3]

Along with becoming more common, adoption is changing in other ways. Until the last twenty or thirty years, the majority of adoptions took place within strict racial, ethnic, and religious lines. White couples adopted white children. Parents with an Italian-American background tended to seek babies whose features, hair color, and skin tones resembled theirs. Catholic families looked for babies born to Catholic women.

Now all that is changing. Interreligious and interracial adoptions are no longer unusual. International adoptions, rare until the last decade or so, are mushrooming. In 1990, Americans adopted 7,093 children from other countries. Within eight years that figure had more than doubled. The majority of international adoptees today come from Russia and China, but hundreds are also arriving from other parts of Asia, as well as Latin America and elsewhere.[4]

Adoptees are changing—and so are the people who adopt. Traditionally, only young married couples with impeccable backgrounds, substantial incomes, neat, clean homes, and conventional religious beliefs bothered even trying to adopt. Such couples are still adopting—witness the Sullums. But older couples are adopting as well. So are unmarried men and women. So are homosexuals, some of them as single parents, others as gay or lesbian couples.

Yet another adoption change has to do with relationships between adoptees and their new families. Once, secrecy was the rule. In the words of a 1963 Illinois law, ". . . adoption severs forever every part of the parent and child relationship. . . . For all legal and practical purposes [an adopted] child is the same as dead to its [biological] parents."[5] By the same legal magic, the adoptive parents treated the child almost as if he or she had been born to them. Adoption papers were locked away and never mentioned. Most adopted children reached adulthood knowing little if anything about their origins. Some were unaware that they had been adopted.

Even today, many people adopted before the 1970s and 1980s cannot tell you much about the infant they once were. "All I know is that I was born in the Bronx," Dan, now in his sixties, told a writer in 1999. "I was born in Ellsworth, Maine, in 1949," said David. Neither man knew anything about his birth parents or whether he had any brothers or sisters. Neither had any idea about his family medical background. Dan's and David's records were permanently sealed (closed) when their adoptions were finalized.

Modern adoptive families are less apt to be so secretive. Some, of course, find secrecy impossible. How would a white American couple go about convincing a child adopted from China or Korea that he had been born to them? But many adoptive families reject secrecy, not because they must, but because they want to. They think it only fair for a child to know about her origins and her birth family's health history at the very least. A growing number of families are opting for more openness in adoption. In an open adoption, birth and adoptive parents either meet in person or communicate about the adoption through a third party. Sometimes birth and adoptive parents remain permanently in touch with one another.

MATTERS OF CONTROVERSY

Not everyone is happy about all the adoption changes. Open adoption may sound like a good idea, but might it seem to an openly adopted young child that he has two sets of parents? Wouldn't that be confusing for him? Adoptees like Dan and David may seek to have their records unsealed in order to learn about their origins—even to locate their birth mothers. Is that fair to the women who agreed to their adoptions so long ago? Birth mothers who relinquish a child generally have good reasons for doing so, and many are determined to remain anonymous. "I don't think it's my child's right to know me," says one woman who gave birth as a single mother and doesn't want anyone to know about it. "I've moved on with my life," she adds. "I don't want someone shoving openness down my throat."[6]

Other people question the wisdom of allowing children to be adopted by anyone other than a stable married couple. Some worry that a single parent may not be able to provide a child with a secure home. Others object to allowing homosexuals to adopt.

Interracial and international adoptions are similarly criticized by some. Children ought to look like the people they call "Mom" and "Dad," some say. Others are dismayed when they see children from countries like China or India being raised in a culture so unlike the one they came from. How will these children learn about their roots?

There is also the matter of the thousands of children still in foster care. What more can be done to get them out of the system and into permanent loving homes?

These are good questions that arise from reasonable doubts. Adoption, and people's ideas about it, change as family life—and ideas about what is best for children—change. We will learn more about those changes throughout this book.

ADOPTIONS PAST 2

Jacob and Michele Sullum adopted Francine Allen because they loved her and didn't want her to end up in foster care. To us, this seems natural, even admirable. Yet only a century ago the idea of adopting a child out of love and concern would have struck many people as odd. That's how much attitudes have changed over the last hundred years. In fact, although adoption has been practiced throughout recorded human history, adoption as we define it—taking a biologically unrelated child who needs a home into one's family through legal means, loving that child, and raising that child as one's own—is a strictly modern phenomenon.

The baby Moses, an early adoptee

ADOPTION IN THE ANCIENT WORLD

The earliest written reference to adoption is found in the code of laws drawn up during the time of Hammurabi, king of Babylon. Hammurabi ruled Babylon—in what is now Iraq—nearly four thousand years ago, during the first half of the eighteenth century B.C.

The Code of Hammurabi makes it clear that Babylonian adoptions were not intended as a means of giving a home to a child in need. Rather, they were carried out for the purpose of providing a childless couple or individual with an heir.

Having an heir was important in Babylon, an agricultural society in which wealthy families cultivated large tracts of land that they handed down from generation to generation. Childless Babylonian artisans—carpenters, goldsmiths, potters—were similarly permitted to adopt.

Adoption in ancient Babylon carried with it distinct advantages. An artisan's adoptee was regarded as an apprentice, legally bound to work alongside the adopter for a set period of time in return for training in his particular line of work. Most birth parents would have been glad to see a child of theirs achieve such a secure future. And any family would have deemed it an honor to have a child adopted as the heir of a rich and powerful personage. Hammurabi's laws also set standards for wet nurses, women hired to feed and care for infants whose mothers had died or who were unable to nurse their babies themselves.

In some ways, the Code of Hammurabi sounds surprisingly modern. Among its concerns: Will the adoptive parents treat an adoptee as they would their biological offspring? Will young adoptees suffer from the change in caregiver? Will adoptee and adoptive parents get along? According to the code, an adoption by an artisan or wealthy landowner remained in force only if the answer to such questions was "yes." If an adoptee was unhappy and "persisted in searching for its father and its mother," the adoption was reversed and the child returned to its birth parents.

Adoptees enjoyed other protections under Hammurabi's laws. Apprentices were bound to their masters as long as they received instruction and remained in line to inherit the trade. If instruction stopped or the inheritance was denied, the adoption could be undone. Wet nurses worked under strict rules and were punished if a child died in their care.

Only those adopted by the most powerful members of Hammurabi's own court were outside the law's protection. "The [adopted] son of a chamberlain . . . shall not be reclaimed," the code says. Even if the adopted son turned out to be unhappy with his new parents, he was not permitted to leave them and rejoin his original family. "If [he] states to the father who has brought him up or the mother who has brought him up, 'Thou art not my father' [or] 'Thou art not my mother,' they shall cut out his tongue."[1] Hammurabi may have had some modern-sounding ideas about harmony within the adoptive family, but when it came to punishments, his attitude was as harsh as anyone else's of his time.

Adoption was common in such other parts of the ancient world as China, India, Greece, and Rome. As in Babylon, adoption in those places was largely for the purpose of obtaining an heir. In

China and India, would-be parents preferred to adopt a member of their own extended family, a nephew or a cousin, perhaps. The parents of a large family would doubtless have been happy to see one of their children being raised by a well-off relative. In China and Rome, adoption was tied to the custom of ancestor worship. In return for the privilege of being adopted into a rich and influential family, the adoptee assumed the duty of tending the shrine dedicated to deceased family members. With that, of course, he would abandon the worship of his own biological ancestors.

Abandoning one set of ancestors in favor of another was a serious step to take, and Roman law reflected that fact. Under laws proclaimed in the eastern part of the Roman Empire in A.D. 529, full adoption was possible only between an adoptee (usually an adult) whose father was dead—and thus unable to reclaim his son—and an adopter who was childless and old enough that he was unlikely to have children of his own.

The laws of 529 also provided for a simpler form of adoption when a prospective adoptee's father was still living. In such cases, the birth father was asked three times if he was willing to forfeit his right to the child. Not until after his third formal relinquishment could the adoption legally occur. Reminders of this ancient law can be seen in the process whereby Evelyn Allen was required to relinquish Francine before the Sullums could adopt her.[2]

KINSHIP FOSTERING

Elsewhere in the world, the transfer of children from one home to another took a very different form. In much of Africa and throughout Oceania, which consists of 25,000 or so islands scattered across the South Pacific Ocean, kinship fostering was the rule. It is estimated that before European-style laws and customs began changing traditional ways of doing things, about 30 percent of children in central Africa and 80 percent of children in Oceania experienced some degree of kinship fostering.

In kinship fostering in Africa and Oceania, children would receive parenting, not only from their mothers and fathers but from numerous other relatives and family friends. A child might stay in one home for a while, then be sent to live in another. Over time she would develop relationships with many adults whom she would regard as parents, and acquire dozens of "brothers," "sisters," and "cousins" her own age.

Kinship fostering evolved as a means of reinforcing people's sense of equality and cementing the loving bonds among them. It is completely different from the kind of adoption for the sake of inheritance or family pride that was common in places like Babylon or Rome. Unlike modern formal adoption, it is not a process that needs to be regulated by law. Above all, it is open. Groups that continue to practice kinship fostering assume that birth parents will share their children. If they refuse to do so, they risk being cut off from friends and relatives. Secrecy would be pointless.[3] Now, as in the past, kinship fostering allows children whose parents have died to be cared for by other family members or friends.

Kinship fostering is practiced by some in the United States and Canada today. It is estimated that nearly four million American children were living in households headed by a grandparent in 1997.[4] If one of these grandparents becomes ill or unable to care for a child, that child may be passed along to another relative for nurturing.

ADOPTION AND MONOTHEISM

Yet another influence on modern adoption dates back to biblical times and the beginnings of monotheism. The word *monotheism* comes from the Greek words "mono," meaning one, and "theism," meaning god. Monotheism is the belief in a single god. Monotheists forbade the worshiping of idols, or objects in nature, or one's own ancestors. The world's leading monotheistic religions, Judaism, Christianity, and Islam, trace their origins back to Abraham, the Old Testament patriarch.

Abraham is believed to have lived around 2100 B.C.[5] Although he lived only a few hundred years before Hammurabi, and in the same part of the world, the attitude toward adoption that emerges from his story as related in the Book of Genesis (not written down until about one thousand years later)[6] is quite unlike the one that permeates ancient Babylonian law. That is partly because life among Abraham's people, the Israelites, was so different from life in Babylon.

The Israelites were nomads who wandered from place to place in search of fresh grazing land for their sheep and goats. They owned no great wealth or vast estates, so having sons to inherit their possessions was not essential to them. In addition, the Israelites were moving toward monotheism. It was Abraham who is said to have promised God that the Israelites would always regard him as their one true

God. As monotheists, the Israelites rejected the ancestor worship that made having direct descendants vital in some other societies. Even so, sons *were* needed to carry on the family name and family traditions.

So it was that Abraham was troubled by the fact that he and his wife Sarah were childless, and he considered adopting a member of his household. However, God expressed displeasure at the idea and promised the couple a child of their own. But none appeared and at Sarah's urging, Abraham eventually had a son by her maid Hagar. (This means of obtaining a son was common in that time and place.)

At first, Abraham and Sarah planned to take Hagar's son, Ishmael, into their home and act as parents to him. But again, God stepped in, once more promising Abraham and Sarah a biological son. Abraham, aware of his great old age, laughed to himself. "Shall *a child* be born unto him that is a hundred years old? And shall Sarah, that is ninety years old, bear?" But to Abraham's astonishment, God kept his promise and Sarah did have a son, Isaac. Abraham's line continued, but in a way that clearly signaled the undesirability of adoption. The Bible made it clear that orphaned children should be taken in and cared for, preferably by a brother of their dead father. But according to those who collected and wrote down the stories and legends that make up the Old Testament, formal adoption merely for the sake of obtaining an heir was not right.[7] (Today, of course, attitudes are different. Modern Jewish couples like Jacob and Michele Sullum are as drawn to adoption as anyone else.)

Islam similarly rejected adoption. Followers of Islam trace their religious roots to Abraham through Ishmael. Islam's holy book, the Koran, condemns adoption even more explicitly than the Old Testament does. "God never put two hearts within one man's body," says the Koran, compiled in A.D. 651–652 (the year 30 in the Islamic calendar). "He does not regard . . . your adopted sons as your own sons." Like the Old Testament, the Koran allows for adoption in the sense of providing homes for children who need them. But, it warns, never pretend that the children so provided for are your own. "Name your adopted sons after their fathers; that is more just in the sight of God," the Koran advises.[8]

Along with finding adoption wrong, traditional Judaism and Islam found it risky. Both the Koran and the Old Testament tell the familiar story of Moses, born in Egypt at a time when the Israelites were being held in slavery there. Orders had gone out from the king, or pharaoh, that all male Israelite babies be slaughtered. Fearing for her child, Moses' mother placed him in a basket and set him adrift in a river. Her hope was that someone would rescue the boy and hire her as his wet nurse.

At first, events went according to plan. Pharaoh's daughter spotted the basket, pulled the baby from the water, and brought him to her parents. Her mother, the queen, liked the look of him. "This child may bring joy to us both," she said to Pharaoh. "Do not slay him. He may show promise, and we may adopt him as our son." Pharaoh agreed, and Moses' own mother was indeed hired to care for him.

But as the Koran puts it, Pharaoh and his wife "little knew what they were doing." Moses grew up rebellious and as a young man he killed an Egyptian whom he had discovered beating an Israelite. Later, God appeared to Moses and ordered him to go to Pharaoh and demand freedom for his people, the Israelites. Moses did just that, to the king's dismay. "Did we not bring you up when you were an infant?" the king wanted to know. "Surely you are ungrateful." He flatly refused to free his slaves.

Moses persisted, however, and God sent terrible plagues intended to persuade Pharaoh to relent and let the Israelites go. In the end, Moses did lead his people out of Egypt. The final blow to his adoptive father came when the waters of the Red Sea miraculously parted so Moses could march the Israelites through to safety—only to come rushing back just in time to drown Pharaoh's entire army.[9]

FEUDAL FAMILIES

Still other ideas about adoption come from the peoples that had inhabited northern Europe since about 6000 B.C. Members of individual clans were related by blood. Each clan was headed by a chief who was chosen by trials of strength; whichever clansman could perform best physically and win the most contests became the leader. Appropriately enough, the chieftain played the role of a stern father keeping his family in order, and his word was law. If he awarded a particular piece of property to a certain clansman, the clansman held that property throughout his lifetime. When a property owner died, it was the chieftain who decided who would inherit. He might give the property to the previous owner's son, but he equally well might not.

There would have been little room in this kind of setup for the formal adoption of either children or adults. Leaders were chosen for their abilities, not their lineage. Since property was disposed of at the will of the chieftain, there was no point in a childless person adopting an heir. Anyway, in a society in which blood ties were of the essence, the adoption of biological strangers would have been considered unacceptable. Informal fostering arrangements, including the taking in of young orphans, would have been easily worked out within the clan.

Centuries passed and by about A.D. 800, European society had evolved into the kind of system we call "feudal." Feudalism grew directly out of the ideas and customs of the old clans. Chieftains—now known as kings or lords—still controlled large estates, or manors. Clansmen and women of lower rank were the king's vassals, his subjects.

Vassals owed absolute loyalty to their lord. To reward that loyalty, the lord handed out land grants, titles of nobility, and other valuables. In a change from earlier times, the ownership of land was largely permanent within a family. Strict rules governed who could inherit. Those rules favored the firstborn son. Leadership positions had also become hereditary. When the king died, the oldest prince assumed the throne. At the lowest level of feudal society were the serfs, or peasants, who worked their master's land and served in his household. Serfs were little more than slaves. They were bound to the land, and few ever ventured from the manor upon which they had been born. Each manor was self-sufficient, a miniature world of its own, producing all the food, clothing, tools, and other necessities its inhabitants needed.

In a feudal society, formal adoption for the sake of gaining an heir was no more necessary or desirable than it had been in previous centuries. Blood ties remained all-important, and inheritance depended upon them. As for orphaned children, they had little trouble finding homes. Living on a manor was like living in a close-knit extended family. Everyone had a secure place in that "family," and someone would always be around to foster an orphaned infant. As soon as they were old enough to perform simple chores, orphans who had been born as serfs would be taken into the lord's household and set to work in the kitchen or the stables. Higher-ranking orphans, infants, or children might find refuge within the Roman Catholic Church. Catholicism was the dominant religion throughout most of Europe in feudal times. Since church leaders did not sanction formal adoption, they felt they needed to provide an alternative means of caring for parentless children. In feudal times and beyond, many orphans passed their childhood in a Catholic religious house, reared by the brothers or sisters who lived there.

A CHANGING WORLD

By the fifteenth century, feudalism had largely broken down in Western Europe. Laws and customs had changed, and serfs were no longer bound to the land as they had once been. Thousands abandoned the countryside and settled in Europe's fast-growing towns and cities. There they encountered a life-style much more open and exciting—and far less certain—than the one they were used to.

The European cities of the fifteenth, sixteenth, and seventeenth centuries were bustling places. Markets flourished and money in the form of coins, all but unknown in feudal times, changed hands readily. The age of capitalism—the economic system under which property is owned by private individuals and goods and services are produced in order to make a profit—had dawned. The self-supporting manor life-style had vanished.

In a capitalist society, says Mary Kathleen Benet, author of *The Politics of Adoption*, children are not an economic asset to their families, as they are in a self-sufficient society. Back on the manor, even three and four year olds could contribute their bit to help feed the family, picking berries, shooing chickens out of the garden, and the like. Between the ages of seven and nine, children became full-time contributors, working the same long hours as adults and doing similar jobs.

It's different in an economy based on money, Benet says. When people must depend upon earning an income to support themselves, children cannot contribute at a meaningful level. Instead of adding to a family's resources, each new child becomes a drain on them. As capitalism took hold across Europe, many parents found it difficult, even impossible, to provide for their children. Some parents abandoned them. Remember the story of Hansel and Gretel? Their fictional abandonment reflected a grim reality.

As society changed, children, orphaned and abandoned alike, roamed the streets, finding food and shelter when and where they could. At the same time, those feudal institutions—the church, the manor and its lord, extended networks of family and friends—that had once cared for children in need were either no longer in place or unable to meet the sharply rising demand for their services. How was society to deal with the problem?

THE POOR LAW AND THE WORKHOUSE

To us, the answer seems simple enough: allow parents to legally surrender the children they cannot care for. Let someone adopt those children and give them a good start in life. But however obvious this solution seems to us, it apparently never occurred to anyone in early modern Europe.

In England especially, the blood ties between parents and their offspring were considered as absolute and unbreakable as they had been in feudal times or in the days of the ancient clans. Formal legal adoption was unknown there, so English lawmakers had to find other ways of handling the problem of homeless children. The way they chose is particularly significant to us, Benet maintains, because the English were to conquer and colonize lands around the globe, imposing their laws and values not only on the United States and Canada but on much of the rest of the world as well.

England's solution turned out to be its Poor Law. In 1597 the country enacted a measure aimed at providing for the destitute of all ages, including children. Under that law, the state took over responsibility for providing for the needy. No longer would it be left to the church or to private individuals to take in the orphaned or abandoned. People unable to care for themselves were to receive relief in the form of food, clothing, and shelter at the expense of the taxpayers of the town or parish in which they lived.

England's Poor Law system, which would remain in place for three hundred years and be altered and added to over that time, sounds more humane than it actually was. True, towns were obliged to assist their poor, but no town wanted to pay out a penny more in relief than it absolutely had to. Each town therefore imposed strict limits and conditions upon those it helped.

Take unmarried mothers and their children. In seventeenth-century England, having an illegitimate child was treated as a religious sin—and a criminal offense. An unwed mother who found herself unable to feed and clothe her child could apply to town officials for aid. If she did, though, those officials would almost certainly take her child from her. (The "unbreakable" blood ties between mother and child did not mean they could not be physically separated in the interests of punishing the mother or "protecting" the child by keeping it from having contact with its sinful parent.) The mother might even be thrown in jail—she had after all committed the crime of having had the child. Faced with such possibilities, how likely was she to ask for help? Or consider a child abandoned by her parents. The town might find someone willing to take her in and feed her. In return, she would almost certainly have been forced to work long and hard as a household servant. She would have had no freedom to come and go as she wished. She could have been beaten or punished in other ways for any hint of disobedience.

Another old story, that of Cinderella, illustrates how a child-servant might have been treated in those times, even by her own stepmother. Rather than accept the fate of a Cinderella, many parentless children took to the street. Some fended for themselves by picking pockets. Others turned to prostitution.

From officialdom's point of view the harsh rules worked well. Even the most desperately needy did everything in their power to avoid falling under the Poor Law. Some mothers managed to find relatives willing to take in a child and care for it. Fostering was a common practice among the poor of England, Benet says, despite the absence of formal adoption. When no fostering arrangement was possible, a mother might leave her infant in the care of a woman who ran a "baby farm." That would free her to try to earn a little money. Many baby farms were overcrowded, squalid places where children received little care and frequently died of starvation or disease. Mothers who left their children on baby farms knew the chance they were taking, but what other choice did they have?

With the 1700s came another Poor Law refinement—the workhouse. Relief officials greeted the innovation enthusiastically. In 1834 they replaced the old system under which individual towns were responsible for their own poor with a nationwide network of workhouses to which the poor could apply for food and shelter.

Family ties meant no more to workhouse authorities than they had to those in charge of the older form of poor relief. Families who turned to a workhouse were immediately split up. Men were housed in a dormitory-style men's building. Women and children under the age of three were sent to a similar women's facility. Children aged three and up were kept apart from their mothers and allowed to see them just four times a year.

As usual under the Poor Law, an important goal of those running workhouses was to make life there so miserable that only the most despairing would turn to one for shelter. Food was meager and clothing rough and shabby. Work was onerous. Jobs, including those given to children, were hard, boring, and often dangerous.

As workhouse children grew, so did their workloads. At the earliest age possible, they were employed—without pay—to help staff the workhouse, an excellent way for those running the place to save the money that would otherwise have gone to hire adult workers. Some children were made to earn their keep by being apprenticed. Others brought in a few coins by being hired out as household servants, farm laborers, and the like. Boys might be forced into the army, navy, or merchant marine, especially when there were shortages in the ranks of those services. Some were assigned to jobs so hazardous that no one else would take them in industries like mining and fishing. Boys and girls alike were shipped off to find ways to support themselves in English colonies around the world.[10]

Exiled to foreign shores, set to work at the most menial of jobs, incarcerated in workhouses, forced into baby farms or dubious fostering arrangements—such, for three centuries, were the fates that awaited England's most desperate children. In America, things were somewhat different.

3
INDENTURE, ASYLUM, ADOPTION

It was in 1742 that eleven-year-old Marguerite Ledoux, along with the uncle and grandmother who were her only living relatives, set out for North America. The three sailed from the port city of Le Havre in France, heading for the French territory called Louisiana. But during the voyage Marguerite's uncle fell ill and died, and by the time the ship docked in the English colony of Massachusetts, her grandmother was too worn out to attempt the difficult journey west and south. Marguerite and her grandmother stayed in lodgings until their money ran out and they were forced to move to the poor farm, a town-run shelter for the indigent. There Marguerite's grandmother died.

An orphan train for relocating orphans

INDENTURE AND APPRENTICESHIP

Marguerite's kinship fostering arrangement was at an end. What was the orphan, penniless and stranded in a foreign land whose language she barely comprehended, to do? Poor-farm authorities had the answer. They would locate a family willing to take her in on condition that she work for them, as long and as hard as they demanded, until her eighteenth birthday.

Marguerite understood English well enough to know exactly what that meant. "She would be answerable to these people for her every act and word, bound to serve them for six long years in return for shelter, food, and such garments as should be deemed necessary."[1] Like so many other New World orphans, she would be legally "bound out" as an indentured servant.

Although Marguerite Ledoux was not a real person—she is a character in the book *Calico Bush* by Rachel Field—the substance of her story is real enough. From colonial times through the 1830s, indenture was the most commonly used means of providing for older orphaned children in English-speaking North America.[2] Very young children would have gone to friends or relatives.

Another way of dealing with New World orphans was to send them into the world as apprentices. This practice, too, has made it into fiction. In Esther Forbes's *Johnny Tremain*, set in Boston on the eve of the American Revolution, Johnny's widowed and dying mother signs a contract of apprenticeship with a master silversmith. When Johnny's mother dies, the twelve year old falls under the terms of the agreement. As the silversmith explains them to Johnny, "I promised to feed and clothe you, keep you in good discipline, and . . . teach you the silversmith's arts and mysteries. . . . And you promised to serve me diligently for seven years. . . ."[3]

That was not such a bad arrangement for an orphan in the America of 1771. Nor was Marguerite Ledoux's future as bleak as it might have been if she had been an orphan in Europe. As we saw in chapter two, there was little room for the orphaned and dependent in crowded Old World cities. European orphans were seen as a burden upon society—unfair though it was—and society treated them harshly as a result.

It was different in the vast open New World. The colonial life-style was largely rural and self-sufficient. There was always work to be done and every willing hand could be put to good use. Since Johnny and Marguerite—and the real-life children whose lives they mirror—were genuinely able to contribute to the society around them, society felt little compulsion to punish them with mean and humiliating living conditions. On the contrary, colonists came to believe that any bright, hardworking young person from a respectable family could get ahead in life. Acting on this belief, colonial authorities tried to see to it that apprentices and indentured servants received at least some education. After the United States won its independence from England, some states required that such children be taught to read and write.[4] Many bound-out children did go on to become prosperous and influential members of their communities.

ASYLUMS AND ORPHAN TRAINS

As the eighteenth century turned into the nineteenth, America changed. In the northeastern states, especially, living conditions increasingly resembled conditions in Europe. Cities were growing. Self-sufficiency was giving way to a monied economy. As had been the case in Europe, an urbanized capitalist society meant an increase in the orphan population. Also as in Europe, the number of orphans was rising at the very same time that the old ways of caring for them—kinship fostering, apprenticeship, and legal indenture—were on the decline. England's response to this dilemma had been the workhouse. America's was the orphan asylum.

The first orphanage in what was to become the United States was opened in 1729 by a group of Catholic nuns in France's Louisiana Territory. A few years later two Protestant orphanages appeared in the English colonies. The only nonreligious, publicly funded orphanage operating in eighteenth century America was in Charleston, South Carolina. This pattern—the state leaving it largely up to private or religious groups to feed, clothe, and shelter needy children—was to continue into the latter part of the nineteenth century.[5]

America's orphanage system grew slowly at first. Then, in 1832 and again in 1849, came outbreaks of a deadly disease: cholera. Each epidemic left numerous orphans and "half orphans," children with only one parent, in its wake. The number of orphanages grew. It grew again following the Civil War (1861–65), which claimed the lives of over three quarters of a million men, many of them fathers of young children. The orphanage system—

which now included state-run asylums—flourished well into the twentieth century. According to U.S. government figures, there were as many as 100,000 orphans, half orphans, and other children living in institutions in 1910.[6] Ten or fifteen years later the number of U.S. orphanages peaked at between 1,300 and 1,350.[7] In addition, children were sometimes sent to orphanages by their parents or guardians on a temporary basis. Orphanage officials might allow destitute parents to place children in their care as an alternative to abandoning them or letting them succumb to semi-starvation and ill health. If and when a family's finances improved, the children would be reclaimed.[8]

Along with orphans, state asylums housed children with what we today call physical, mental, and emotional disabilities. Other inmates were delinquent—by the standards of the day at any rate. As late as the early twentieth century, children could be locked up in adult jails or asylums for such offenses as vagrancy, hunting on private land, school truancy, even playing on revolving doors.[9]

Orphanage life was strenuous. Inmates were expected to earn their keep, working in the orphanage kitchen or laundry, cleaning dormitories, raising food crops, and the like. In addition they might be required to work outside the orphanage, as seasonal farm laborers, for instance, handing over their hard-won wages to help pay orphanage expenses.

Although American orphanages were not deliberately designed to brutalize, as English workhouses had been, they were dreary places in which to grow up. The orphanage system was based upon inflexible routine and uniformity, and orphanage children led suffocating lives. Still another fictional orphan, Judy Abbott in Jean Webster's *Daddy-Long-Legs*, complained that the aim of the asylum in which she grew up was "to turn . . . ninety-seven orphans into ninety-seven twins."[10] Webster, who believed the orphanage system badly needed reforming, wrote *Daddy-Long-Legs* in 1912 partly in order to draw public attention to the deadening effects of asylum life.

Despite the number of institutions, the orphanage system never even succeeded in serving more than a fraction of America's orphans. In 1910, when over 1,100 asylums were operating around the country, it is estimated that 25,000 homeless children were wandering the streets of New York City alone.[11] Many scraped by on their own, sleeping in alleys or open spaces and begging for food and money or doing odd jobs to earn both. Others faced "rescue" by organizations like the Children's Aid Society.

The Children's Aid Society was founded in New York in 1853 for the purpose of relocating urban orphans to rural settings. That meant rounding up homeless children—orphans, half orphans, and the merely destitute—loading them aboard freight trains, and shipping them out West. There they were claimed by men and women who wanted a bit of extra help around the house, farm, or shop. In all, as many as 200,000 children may have been moved from city to country between the 1850s and the 1920s.[12]

To this day, the Orphan Train effort remains controversial. Was it a noble effort to help orphans find good homes? Or was it the callous abandonment of desperate children to what could turn out to be a harsh fate?

For Arthur Field it was the former. Arthur was five when he scrambled off an Orphan Train and onto a man's lap. "Are you going to be my daddy?" Arthur asked. The man, who had come to the train station only out of curiosity, was captivated. He took the boy home to stay. Field reminisced happily about his childhood at a May 2000 reunion of Orphan Train veterans. But another man at the reunion, William Oser, recalled that he and his sister were severely abused by their adoptive parents.[13]

Even as the Orphan Trains continued to roll westward and the orphanage system expanded, the end of both was in sight. That end came about thanks to new ways of thinking about the very nature of childhood.

THE ADOPTION ALTERNATIVE

By the late 1800s, people were coming to realize that children are not simply small people who can be treated like adults. They are *children,* human beings with specific requirements that change with age. Infants need lots of physical affection and attention. Older children need stable homes, loving discipline, encouragement, and plenty of time to play and explore on their own. Then there are teenagers.

The concept of adolescence as a distinct time of life, separate from either childhood or adulthood, was only just emerging in the early twentieth century. Teenagers have specialized needs, too, a new breed of professional child care experts declared. In the case of orphaned teens, those needs were being met neither in the stultifying orphanage nor by the questionable methods of groups like the Children's Aid Society.

Gradually, the new ideas transformed the way orphans and other children in need were treated. Disabled children whose parents could not care for them were no longer banished to orphanages, but sent to institutions equipped to meet their particular requirements. Truants and mischief makers were encouraged to join new organizations like the YMCA or the Boy Scouts and Girl Scouts or Big Brothers and Big Sisters, while genuine delinquents were funneled into recently formed state juvenile justice systems.[14]

Even the children of the desperately poor who rotated between institutions and their own homes began disappearing from the orphanage scene. In the 1910s, states started offering relief payments to the destitute mothers of some children, enabling those mothers to keep their youngsters at home. (Such relief went to white mothers only; racial prejudice kept blacks from benefiting from early state aid programs.)[15] In the 1930s, the federal government established its own Aid to Dependent Children (ADC) program, further cutting into the orphanage's role as temporary refuge.

The effect of all these social changes was to bring about a change in the population of children needing homes. ADC and other relief programs meant that more of the children of poverty-stricken parents could stay with their biological families. Children who had committed crimes were now housed in juvenile jails rather than in adult prisons or asylums. Children with disabilities were beginning to receive the kind of therapy and rehabilitation services they needed. Thus, more and more of the children still living in orphanages were healthy youngsters with birth mothers prepared to relinquish their parental rights—prime candidates for placement in the kind of permanent adoptive homes familiar to us today.

And by now, modern adoption was an idea whose time had come. Already, back in 1851, Massachusetts had enacted the first adoption law in the English-speaking world. The Massachusetts statute was also the first in modern times to consider the welfare of the child to be adopted as well as the rights of the adoptive family.[16]

Twenty-three years later Michigan took another step toward modern adoption, passing a law that put some homeless children there into temporary state custody. The Michigan law also authorized agents appointed by the governor to seek out suitable private homes in which those children would be welcomed, not as servants, but as members of the family.

Within twenty-five years, similar child placement programs had been established in nine other states. By 1914, the National Home Finding Society, whose goal was to locate permanent homes for as many orphans as possible, boasted thirty-two state chapters.[17]

It was also in 1914 that World War I began in Europe. That war, which ended in 1918, prompted a dramatic shift in public attitudes toward adoption.

ADOPTION CATCHES ON

As World War I began, the German army invaded the small nation of Belgium, shooting, burning, shelling—and creating thousands of orphaned and homeless children in the process. News photos of the children's frightened, forlorn faces touched hearts everywhere. Suddenly the fact that there were children in need of homes was on everyone's mind. Offers to adopt poured in from America and even from England, where adoption had always been considered suspect and laws regulating the practice were not yet on the books.

To their chagrin, would-be adopters soon learned that Belgians would rather care for their own orphans than send them off to be raised by foreigners. Social workers in England and America reminded disappointed couples that there were plenty of native-born orphans in both countries. Why not open their homes to *those* children? Couples—especially childless couples—responded eagerly. Adoption rates climbed, and in 1926 England passed its first-ever adoption law.[18]

NEW ADOPTION LAWS

New adoption laws took effect in the United States and Canada as well. The laws varied from state to state and province to province. Variations continue, although federal guidelines are in place to govern cross-country adoptions.

Overall, the intent of the early twentieth-century laws was to match newborns who needed homes with couples who were unable to have biological children. Further goals were ensuring that babies were placed in the best possible homes available, while couples got those infants most suited to them and to their family backgrounds.

To social workers and legislators of the day, achieving those goals meant drawing up rules aimed at placing youngsters exclusively with happily married, well-educated, religiously observant, middle- or upper-income, law-abiding, mentally and physically healthy legal citizens who, though not able to produce children of their own, were still young enough to have been the child's actual birth parents. It also meant pairing adoptive parents and adoptees in terms of such factors as race and religion.

To make sure everyone followed the rules, lawmakers sought to funnel adoptions through public or private social welfare agencies. Today most states also allow private, or independent, adoptions. Private adoptions are arranged by someone in a position to know both a couple longing for a child and a mother with a baby she feels unable to care for herself. Such a person, often a doctor, lawyer, or member of the clergy, acts as an intermediary between birth and adoptive parents. Like other adoptive couples, those who adopt independently must undergo a home study by a qualified professional and have the adoption finalized in a court of law.[19] Independent adoptions account for as many as 80 percent of all adoptions of U.S.-born adopted children today.[20]

In many ways the new rules served parents and children well. They definitely represented an improvement over asylum life or the kind of adoptions arranged by the Children's Aid Society and similar organizations. A birth mother who felt compelled to agree to an adoption could be reasonably sure that her child would find a good home. Adoptive parents liked hearing that they were getting a healthy child whose biological mother wanted only the best for him or her. Adoptees grew up being told that they were "special" children, "chosen" above all others by their new parents. During much of the twentieth century, adoptive families flourished throughout the United States and Canada.

QUESTIONABLE LAWS AND PRACTICES

Yet for all their good intentions, many of today's adoption experts say, some adoption rules and practices were flawed.

To begin with, they were racially biased. The United States—and to a lesser extent, Canada—has a long cruel history of racism. Until the 1950s most agencies refused even to consider interracial adoption. The practice was illegal in some southern states.[21] As a result, black infants were far more likely to languish in orphanages than white infants because there were fewer black families in a position to provide adoptive homes than whites.

Early adoption laws also were rigid with regard to religion. Many private adoption agencies were affiliated with Catholic, Protestant, or Jewish groups and refused to surrender any of their children to interfaith adoption. Better to let children remain unadopted and in orphanages than allow them to be raised in a religion other than the one into which they had been born.

But of all the flaws to be found in older adoption laws and practices, the most devastating was their insistence upon privacy, a privacy so complete that it amounted to a thick wall of secrecy.

Secrecy Rules There were reasons for the secrecy wall. To begin with, consider the concerns of the adoptive parents. Most turned to adoption because they had failed to conceive and did not want to share that information with the world at large. Nowadays, few infertile couples hesitate to discuss their condition openly. Many go so far as to appear on radio or television to share their thoughts and feelings with nationwide audiences. Yet only a few years ago infertility was regarded as an embarrassing personal secret. That made a couple's reason for adopting a secret, too. For some, the adoption itself became part of the secret. Family and close friends may have known about it, but the rest of the world did not. In some instances, not even the child would be told that he or she was adopted.

Another important reason for privacy was to protect the birth mother from public scrutiny. Most were of high school or college age—and unmarried. Having an illegitimate child in mid-twentieth-century America was not a crime as it had been in the past, but neither was it treated as casually as it is today. Thirty or so years ago, pregnancy outside of marriage was seen as shameful. With abortion illegal until the 1970s, an unmarried mother-to-be had little choice but to endure that shame—quit school or her job, drop out of sight, have the baby as unobtrusively as possible, and give it up for adoption at once, sometimes without ever having seen it. Then she would resume her normal life and no one, perhaps not even her future husband and children, would know about her past. That was the idea, anyway.

Carol Schaefer remembers what it felt like being pregnant and unmarried in the 1960s. She was whisked away to a home for unwed mothers and ordered to use the building's back door so no one would see her comings and goings and guess her secret. Schaefer was not even allowed to reveal her last name to other girls and women at the home. (A made-for-television movie, *The Other Mother*, based on Schaefer's story about her later search for her birth son, airs regularly on NBC-TV.)[22]

Besides shielding adoptive parents and unmarried birth mothers, the privacy rules were intended to protect the infants surrendered for adoption. Lawmakers and social workers reasoned that the infants needed that protection because society had traditionally shunned illegitimate children and their mothers. Only if the fact of their illegitimacy could be concealed would adoptees be valued as highly as children born to married couples. Thus it seemed to be in everyone's best interests to veil adoption in secrecy: Issue the adoptee a new birth certificate with the names of the birth parents replaced by those of the adoptive parents; seal the adoption records safely away; and proclaim to all that the new adoptive family is no different from any other family.

But it *is* different, insists Betty Jean Lifton, an adoption expert. Anyone who says otherwise is playing what she calls the Adoption Game of As If.

Adoption "As If" In this game, Lifton maintains, "The adoptive parents embrace the child *as if* it were of their own blood and ask the child to live *as if* this were true." Parents who play the game of As If, Lifton says, may find themselves lying to their adopted child in order to protect the child—and the adoptive family itself.[23]

Others agree. Adoptive families *are* different from biological ones, says Elizabeth Bartholet, a professor of law at Harvard University and the mother of two adopted sons. There is nothing wrong with that, she adds, but adoption laws are written in ways that make it seem as if there were. Those laws treat adoptive families, not just as different but as second-rate. By requiring the rewriting of records and enforcing secrecy, Bartholet maintains, the law suggests that adoptive families are more fragile, more likely to fall apart, than biological families.[24] In that, the law reflects ancient English and American doubts about the validity of adoption and the overwhelming importance of blood ties.

Lifton knows how it feels to be raised As If. Adopted as an infant, she grew up with questions about her birth parents. Her adoptive mother supplied answers. Lifton's birth father had died from war injuries when she was an infant, she told the child, and her heartbroken mother soon followed him. It was a romantic tale, as Lifton now knows, one intended to shield her from a less glamorous reality—that her biological mother had been an unmarried seventeen year old.[25] But it was also a lie, one meant to convince Lifton that her birth parents were dead and gone, out of the picture for all time. That lie, Lifton believes, was an adoptive mother's way of trying to make sure her daughter would never go looking for her biological family. Because if she did go looking, and found her birth parents, wouldn't the ties of blood turn out to be more compelling than those of adoption? Wouldn't her adoptive parents risk losing the child they had loved and raised? Lifton herself knew that the answers were "no." She was happy with her adoptive parents. But Lifton's adoptive mother was sure the answers were "yes." The fear of losing a child to his or her biological family plagues many adoptive parents.

Throughout childhood, Lifton accepted her adoptive mother's account without question. Its tragedy haunted her imagination. "[I] lived with ghostly shadows in my room and the conviction that I too would die young," she says.

Lifton has met other adoptees of the 1930s, 1940s, and 1950s who have similarly been visited by ghosts and fears with no basis in reality. One girl grew up being told—falsely—that her mother had died in childbirth. As an adult, the girl was convinced that she would also die if she had a child. Another adoptee was informed that her birth parents had perished in a car crash on their way home from the hospital where she was born. When her younger brother, also adopted, appeared on the scene, the story was that his parents had died in an airplane crash. The lies left that woman with a crippling fear of travel.

Naturally, adoptive parents did not mean to frighten their children with invented stories. Most who told such stories did so on the advice of the adoption experts and social workers of the day. Those experts believed that the best way to help adopted children flourish in their new homes was to encourage them to put the past firmly behind them and to regard their adoptive family as their only "real" family. Of course not all adoptive parents followed the social workers' advice. Some made a point of being completely forthright about the adoption.

Lifton also spoke with adoptees who recalled being told by their adoptive parents that those parents had chosen them specifically, out of all the other children they could have adopted. Often, these "chosen baby" stories are true. Jacob and Michele Sullum certainly chose to adopt Francine Allen. But Lifton asserts that adoptive parents can unknowingly mislead a child with such a story.

For example, young children may get the impression that their adoptive parents went to a sort of giant nursery and picked them out of all the other children there. As a woman named Grace told Lifton, "I had visions of Mom and Dad walking down a very sterile room . . . and two hundred bawling babies in their tiny cribs." But as Grace reconstructed the event, her parents chose her for all the wrong reasons. "I imagined they stopped and took one glance at me and decided I looked like I needed the most help. I probably looked like a drowned rat." Grace, however happy she was with her adoptive family, cannot have taken much comfort from this particular chosen baby story.

What is more, chosen baby stories are as likely as any other story adoptees hear to be fabrications. As Grace learned as an adult, she had not been chosen—her adoptive parents took her in when another family member gave birth to a baby she couldn't care for. Grace's birth mother turned out to be a woman she grew up believing to be her aunt. Her "cousins" were actually her brothers and sisters.

Chosen baby stories and other fictions adoptive parents use to sustain the As If can backfire in other ways, Lifton and other adoption experts agree. By age seven or eight, a child is old enough to realize that if someone chose to be his mother, someone else chose not to be. Knowing that your birth mother, the one person in the world who should love you more than anyone else, was willing to give you away would be enough to make any child feel anxious and depressed. Reassurances—"She let you go so you could have a better life." "She did it because she loved you so much." "It must have taken a lot of courage to say goodbye."—may be true, but they may not be enough to erase the pain. Betty Jean Lifton is married and has had children. She has led a successful and satisfying life as a psychologist, a writer, and an internationally known authority on adoption. Yet earlier in her life she says, she sometimes felt like an "imposter . . . a helpless changeling . . . " who sensed "the darkness" within.[26]

It was in the hope of lifting that sense of darkness that Lifton undertook to find out who she was and what the circumstances around her birth had been.

4

SEARCHES AND OPEN ADOPTION

Thinking about it today, Betty Jean Lifton finds it hard to remember how "outrageous" and "radical" it was considered for an adoptee to search for her birth mother back when she did it in the 1950s. In those days, the very idea that anyone would begin such a Search—Lifton spells the word with a capital letter—was so unlikely that a social worker at the agency that had handled Lifton's adoption hesitated only a moment before giving Lifton's birth mother's name to her husband. "[T]he agency trusted us since my husband is a psychiatrist," Lifton explains in *Twice Born: Memoirs of an Adopted Daughter*, the book she later wrote about her Search. Perhaps the social worker assumed that anyone with psychi-

*An adoptee with her adoptive father's blessing
reunites with her birth mother.*

atric training would be capable of making his wife see the foolishness of trying to find the mother who had given her up for adoption.

THE SEARCH

But Lifton's husband was already committed to helping her in her Search. Armed with her birth mother's name (Rachel Rosenblatt) and hometown (Providence, Rhode Island), Lifton was almost ready to begin looking. Before she took the big step, though, she wanted advice from someone who would be more objective than a husband. She made an appointment with another psychiatrist.

"Neurotic"—that was how the psychiatrist characterized Lifton's wish to find her birth mother. "The biological mother is unimportant in a case like this," she went on. "The only reason you want to find her is that you did not have a good relationship with your adoptive one." Lifton protested that that was not true. She loved her adoptive mother; she just wanted to know her birth parent as well. But the doctor persisted. "Your mother may not even want to see you. . . . This could be very unpleasant for your mother." The doctor predicted that if Lifton did succeed in finding her birth mother she would not be satisfied unless she found her birth father as well. "Her tone clearly implied," Lifton wrote, that this man would turn out to be thoroughly undesirable—a "madman, murderer, rapist."[1]

Lifton is not the only adoptee who has heard dire warnings before beginning a Search. A woman named Karla questioned the doctor who had delivered her about her mother. The doctor was reluctant to supply information. He suggested that Karla's mother might have "made a good life for herself

57

with a fine husband and children who know absolutely nothing of her past." It wouldn't help anyone to intrude upon the happy family. Or, the doctor went on, obviously recalling that this was an illegitimate birth he was talking about, "suppose that she has sunk even lower on the social scale— that she has become a lifetime tramp." Would knowing that make Karla feel better? If the woman is a tramp perhaps she will see her daughter as "a potential for blackmail benefits." Another adoptee, Martha, heard equally blunt remarks from an adoption professional. "They didn't want you then," the social worker said, "they wouldn't want you now."

The one person with whom Lifton absolutely could not discuss her Search was her adoptive mother. That mother had made her promise to keep her adoption a secret even before embarking upon the pretty lies about the wounded soldier and his tragic widow. Although she was no longer a child, Lifton felt her adoptive mother would fear that a living birth mother might replace her in her adopted daughter's affections. In the 1950s, most experts agreed that sparing an adoptive parent that fear was reason enough for adoptees to forget about looking for their birth parents. As late as 1977, when Searches were becoming common, one therapist and adoptive mother compared an adoptee's desire to undertake a Search to a young child's penchant for lying or stealing. "Maturity comes when we learn to control such impulses," Eda LeShan declared in an article in *Woman's Day* magazine.[2]

Lifton, however, was determined to find her birth mother and she did. The two met twice in person and talked often on the telephone. But the relationship was strained. Lifton still could not talk to her adoptive mother about her birth family and she had always kept the fact of her adoption a secret from her own two children. Not until Lifton's twelve-year-old son chose to write her biography as a homework assignment did she reluctantly reveal the truth.

Rachel Rosenblatt had secrets, too. She was married now, to her second husband. She had a son, Lifton's younger half brother, by her first husband. She was determined to keep them from ever knowing about her illegitimate daughter. Lifton was forbidden—taboo—in her birth mother's everyday life. It would be years before Lifton would manage to cajole her birth mother into revealing her birth father's name.[3]

Things are very different today. According to E. Wayne Carp, a professor of history in Washington state and author of *Family Matters: Secrecy and Disclosure in the History of Adoption*, fully one third of adoptees seek their birth parents. Of these, 80 percent are women.[4]

Why the change? Part of the answer has to do with the various "rights" movements of the 1960s and 1970s. During those years black Americans were demanding—and getting—laws that guaranteed their right to vote and to use such public facilities as swimming pools and drinking fountains. Women were demanding the right to work at jobs once reserved exclusively for men. College students were demanding the right to have more say in what courses they took and how their schools were run. Adoptees believed they, too, had a right—the right to learn the most basic facts about who they were. Many began speaking up.

CHANGING ATTITUDES

Slowly, social workers and others retreated before the demands for increased adoption openness. In 1976 the Child Welfare League of America conducted a study of social welfare agency attitudes toward adoption secrecy in the United States and Canada. It was the league that had, in 1938, issued the guidelines that called for the rewriting of birth certificates and the severing of all ties between adoptees and their birth parents. In 1968, the league had formally reaffirmed its privacy guidelines.

"But times have changed," league research associate Mary Ann Jones noted in a report summarizing the results of the 1976 survey. Although the survey found that 90 percent of the agencies that responded to the league's questionnaire were still assuring both birth and adoptive parents that privacy would be maintained, most were more willing than they had once been to share information under certain circumstances. Several allowed biological parents to place in the record a statement of willingness to hear from a birth child interested in finding them. Many permitted the release of non-identifying information—facts about an adoptee's family health history or his or her ethnic background, for example. The report also noted a "groundswell" of support for the idea that adoptees "have a right to know the full details of their past, including the identity of their natural parents."[5]

Today the groundswell continues. One way it manifests itself is through the growing number of so-called "reunion registries" in the United States and Canada. Registries are places where adoptees can go in hopes of learning more about themselves than the nonidentifying facts they hear from adoption agency social workers. Adoptees hoping to locate a birth parent, however, should be aware that registries do not release information that would lead to the identification of a birth parent who does not want to be found. Only if a birth parent has given permission will registry officials part with information that could lead to a meeting. Many parents do give permission. Some adoptees are delighted to learn that a birth parent has already been in touch with a registry and is hoping for a face-to-face encounter. Reunion registries limit their services to adoptees who are adults—over the age of eighteen or twenty-one. Some are privately operated; others are run by the state or province in which they are located. Many are to be found on the Internet[6]—a powerful new tool that more and more adoptees are utilizing in their Searches.

It was almost by accident that Rhonda Nabors found her birth parents in cyberspace. Nabors, of Grand Prairie, Texas, knew her birth parents' names. She also knew that her father had studied art in college and that he and her mother, both of whom had grown up in Los Angeles, had wanted to teach. Over the years she had looked for their names in phone books and consulted groups that help adoptees look for their biological families. Nothing turned up. Then one day in 1998, Nabors was reading a favorite comic strip online. The Web site offered biographical information about the strip's creator who—coincidentally, Nabors thought—had the same last name as her birth father.

The coincidences mounted. Nabors learned that the cartoonist was from Los Angeles and that he and his wife were teachers. Nabors sent an e-mail. "I am going to be straight to the point," she typed. "I think I may be your daughter." She was. The artist and his wife—Nabors' birth mother—had married after Nabors was adopted. Later they had two other children, Nabors' full siblings.[7]

Dan, whom we met briefly in chapter one, deliberately turned to the Internet in late 1999 in search of information about possible biological siblings. Dan was sixty when the last elderly member of his adoptive family passed away and he began thinking about his birth family and wondering if he had any brothers or sisters. "I couldn't have looked for them when my parents were alive," he says. "They couldn't have handled it."

Unsure whether he wanted to meet family members, or just find out if any existed, Dan proceeded slowly. His first step was locating the agency through which he had been adopted. That done, he went online and found an investigator who specialized in tracking down original birth certificates and the names that go with them.

Did Dan want to go ahead and hire the man? Suddenly he did. "I just got mad," he says now. "I realized that someone out there had all that information about me and didn't even care about it. I care and I want to know! That information is mine." Two weeks later the investigator called to tell Dan that although his birth parents had died he had a living older brother—who had grown up with his birth parents—and an even older half brother who had been raised by other relatives. The next day Dan learned to his astonishment that he had yet another full brother. That brother, younger than

Dan, had also been adopted outside the family. Amazingly none of his three siblings had known anything about Dan—or each other. Dan's uncle, just seventeen years old and sworn to silence when Dan was born, felt nothing but relief when Dan reintroduced himself to the family. "I kept that secret for sixty-two years," he marveled.

REUNIONS

Dan and his older brother Bob promptly made plans to meet. But will they and their families become close? As one adoptee points out, "Reunion is just the first step of a very long journey." That journey, adds another, is "different for different people."[8]

Many Reunions (another word that those involved with adoption capitalize) do lead to satisfying long-term relationships. Rhonda Nabors, along with her husband and three children, visit regularly with her birth family. Raychel Ella Wade was in her mid-twenties when she found her birth mother in 1998. During the course of their Reunion, Wade asked her mother about the man who was her father. He and her mother had never married and had not seen or heard from each other in years, but the older woman knew where to find him. All three began getting together and a year later, Raychel Wade was an attendant at her birth parents' wedding.[9]

In other cases, relationships are less easily resolved. Kerry Anne Herlihy was twenty-seven and living in New York City when she made contact with her birth mother, whose home was in the Midwest. Mother and daughter agreed that Herlihy would fly to St. Louis, Missouri, where they would meet for lunch near the airport. Aware that her existence was unknown to anyone other than her mother's husband (who was not her birth father), Herlihy wondered during their hour-long Reunion whether her mother was worried about being seen by someone she knew. "I get a thrill out of being a real, live secret," she wrote, reliving the experience. "It gives me an edge knowing that I embody someone's sordid past." Thrilling perhaps, but surely feeling part of a "sordid past" must be unsettling, too. A couple of weeks later Herlihy received a letter from her birth mother: "Dear Kerry, . . . you've been in my thoughts. . . . I'm still overwhelmed. . . such a joy and blessing. . . . My thoughts and feelings are still a bit jumbled. . . ."[10] Herlihy and her mother may come to terms with their situation, although it could take time. But a Colorado woman saw her Reunion hopes come crashing down around her when the father she had longed for and eventually found refused to have anything to do with her.[11] Such rejection is painful, and fear of it is one reason an adoptee may decide against beginning a Search.

Another reason for delaying a Search—or avoiding one altogether—stems from an adoptee's fear of hurting his or her adoptive parents. Kerry Anne Herlihy's adoptive mother kept her emotional distance from her daughter's Search. She was aware that Herlihy was flying out to meet her birth mother, but she did not want to hear details about their encounter. Loving her adoptive mother dearly, Herlihy kept those details to herself. Dan knew that his adoptive parents would have been distraught if he had initiated a Search. With their feelings in mind, he had never mentioned the subject to them.

However successful or unsuccessful any individual Reunion is, one thing seems certain. There are going to be more of them. Legal changes and challenges to the old rules of confidentiality will see to that.

MEASURE 58

As 1999 began, laws in forty-six of the fifty states protected adoption privacy by requiring that all records, including original birth certificates, be permanently sealed. Only in Alaska, Delaware, Kansas, and Tennessee did adoptees have access to those records. Voters in a fifth state, Oregon, were about to decide on a measure that would allow adult adoptees to obtain their original birth certificates, complete with the names of their biological parents, without having to scour the Internet or track down old documents in an exhaustive Search. Oregon's Measure 58, as it was called, passed.

Measure 58 had a host of supporters. One, sixty-eight-year-old adoptee Bob Whalley, planned to use it to learn more about his health background—and that of his children. Whalley has heart and lung problems. "What I really want is the medical background, whether my own kids could inherit some condition we should know about," he says.[12] Like many others, Whalley believes that adoptees have a right to know as much about their health as nonadopted people do. He is aware, of course, that agencies collect health histories from birth parents who agree to an adoption and that many agencies are willing to share that nonidentifying information with the adoptee. But agency records vary in their thoroughness and some health problems don't manifest themselves until people reach middle age. Unless the birth parents continuously update agency files, important information could be missing. Besides, reading a few general facts about one's parents' health is not the same as hearing in detail how an uncle's diabetes developed or finding out that several cousins have a form of cancer that tends to run in families.

Adoptees can benefit in other ways from contact with biological relatives. Dan learned that his grandparents had hailed from Russia and Austria, and he heard family stories from his brother Bob. For the first time in his life he had a sense of his own personal heritage. For many adoptees, not having access to their own personal heritage creates a huge void. At the same time, Dan experienced a new feeling of gratitude toward his adoptive parents. "They gave me so many advantages," he says.

Betty Jean Lifton learned the truth about why her birth mother had decided on adoption and she came to sympathize with the difficulties that had forced that decision. Lifton felt a "deeper understanding" of her adoptive mother as well.[13] Rhonda Nabors recognized the source of her son's budding talent as a cartoonist to be her birth father (his biological grandfather).

Nor are adoptees alone in gaining new insights when they reunite with biological family members. Dan's brother Bob suddenly understood why his father had objected so strongly when he and his wife considered naming one of their sons Andrew. Dan's birth name was Andrew. Having to use that name for a grandson would have been a constant painful reminder for the older man. Both Bob and Dan felt closer to the father only one of them had known as they pieced together bits of his emotional history.

Perhaps most important for adoptees, supporters of Oregon's Measure 58 suggest, is the psychological relief they feel when they have uncovered their origins and are no longer plagued by a sense of not knowing who they are. It was that sense of anonymity that Betty Jean Lifton reflected when she called herself an "imposter" or "changeling." It is what another adoptee was thinking of as she told Lifton, "When you don't know how you were born, you don't exist. It muddles everything." That feeling of not really existing led a sixteen-year-old Canadian adoptee to describe herself as having been "hatched," rather than born. "And it really blew her mind," the psychologist to whom the girl made this remark reported, "when I said 'You had a father and a mother even if you don't know anything about them.'" Lifton understands the girl's bewilderment. Unlike other people, adoptees are not told that they look just like Great-Aunt Ellen or that they have their father's good business sense. They do not hear stories about their mothers' pregnancies or that last-minute rush to the hospital. All they hear about is being chosen. Lacking an original birth certificate, she goes on, only adds to the feeling of having been adopted, but not born.[14]

THE OPPOSITION

For all the support Measure 58 garnered, there was opposition as well. As soon as the measure passed, six Oregon women, each a birth mother who had given a child up for adoption, asked the courts to declare it invalid.

The women—whose names were not made public—argued that the law invaded their right to privacy. Each had gone through the adoption process on the understanding that no one would ever know about it. Doctors, lawyers, clergymen, and social workers had assured them that their secret would be safe for all time. "We made life decisions based on those assurances," one of the birth mothers wrote in an unsigned article. "Soon, for $15 [the cost of acquiring a birth certificate], the state may simply hand over your identity to the adult you placed for adoption as an infant 21-plus years ago. . . . [T]he very promises we built our lives upon may be up for sale."[15]

Birth mothers had other concerns. "What about a rape victim who gave up her child—why would she want to revisit the rape?" asks one.[16] Reawakening old memories could be equally traumatic for mothers whose children were born as a result of incest, or while they were in an abusive relationship.

The birth mothers had their sympathizers, even among the adopted. "I do see [their] point of view," said Berry Price. Price was the result of his birth mother's "indiscretion" while her husband was serving overseas during World War II (1939–1945). Wanting to keep her husband from learning about the birth of her child, she agreed to allow the infant to be adopted. Price can understand why his mother—if still living—might not want him suddenly showing up on her doorstep. "But what about me?" he asks. Price hoped to obtain his birth certificate and locate the siblings he knows he must have.[17]

Opposition to Measure 58 also came from a number of men and women who argue against a pregnant woman's right to have an abortion. Many antiabortion activists fear that unsealing the records will lead more women to choose abortion instead of adoption. Unless an unmarried pregnant woman has an ironclad guarantee that no one will ever know about her illegitimate child, they predict, she will decide that abortion is her only option.[18]

Not everyone agrees. Attitudes toward illegitimacy and unwed motherhood are very different now than in the past, many say. Unmarried celebrities and their toddlers smile from the pages of glossy family-oriented magazines. New mothers proudly announce their babies' births in the pages of local newspapers. Sometimes the father's name also appears; sometimes the mother's stands alone. Thousands of unmarried women in the United States and Canada feel comfortable raising their children by themselves. Until her death in 1996, Francine Allen Sullum's birth mother was one of them. Society's growing acceptance of single mothers, many believe, means that there will be no great rise in abortion rates even if adoption is no longer veiled in secrecy.

Still others with objections to Measure 58 included adoptive parents who, like Lifton's mother, feared losing their place in their adopted child's life. It came as well from adoptees eager to protect their adoptive parents. One such adoptee wrote an indignant letter to the editor of *The New York Times* after reading about the Measure 58 controversy in that newspaper. "Where in this debate is consideration given to adoptive parents?" she wanted to know. If original birth certificates are made available, she warned, "adoptive parents become little more than temporary caretakers."[19]

There is evidence, however, that support for this position is slipping. A study conducted by researchers at Cornell University in Ithaca, New York, looked at 1,274 adoptive parents in 743 adoptive homes throughout the state. The findings, released in 1996, showed "overwhelming" support for opening adoption records. "Eighty-three percent of adoptive mothers and 73 percent of adoptive fathers felt that adult adoptees should be able to obtain a copy of their original birth certificates," the report says. Just 11 percent of adoptive fathers and 9 percent of adoptive mothers were opposed to opening adoption records. "There is no justification for keeping such information from adult adoptees," concludes Cornell's Rosemary Avery, who headed the study. "And there is no reason to believe that New York state adoptive parents are any different from those in other states."[20]

The Measure 58 controversy came to an end in May 2000. A month earlier, the Oregon Supreme Court had ruled against the birth mothers. In May the U.S. Supreme Court refused to hear the mothers' case and at that the law went into effect. Bob Whalley, Berry Price, and the more than 2,200 other Oregonians who had applied to see their birth certificates were set to begin their Searches.[21] The battle over opening adoption records moved on to other locales.

Open-record advocates are determined to win their case. At bottom, they argue, their cause is a matter of adoptees' rights as citizens and human beings.

Arthur Wallace, a California medical doctor, summed up the argument in a letter to *The New York Times*. Of course a birth certificate has important psychological meaning, he wrote. It is a "pathway to an understanding of where [a person comes] from . . . a document that tells one's roots, origin, and the truth of one's heritage." But it is also, he pointed out, "a public record." As such, it cannot fairly be withheld from the very person it most deeply concerns.

"Adoptees are identical to nonadopted people except in their rights to public information," Wallace wrote. "Denying access to a public record [the birth certificate] to a group of people [adoptees] is discrimination. . . . When adopted babies grow up and become adults, they should have the same rights as all the rest of us grown-ups."[22]

OPEN ADOPTION

Akin to the debate over privacy is the concern over open adoption.

"There is no one definition of an open adoption," Colleen Alexander-Roberts, an expert in parenting issues, writes in her book, *The Legal Adoption Guide*. Broadly, the term refers to an adoption process in which there is some measure of contact between the birth parents and the adoptive ones. In a semiopen adoption, the contact may be limited to a preadoption exchange of letters and photos. Alternatively, it might involve a brief first-names-only meeting at a lawyer's office or some other neutral location. In such a case, any post-adoption relationship between the two sets of parents will probably be conducted through an intermediary.

In a fully open adoption, first and last names and home addresses are exchanged. A wide range of information—not just about health and family background but also about hobbies, musical tastes, favorite sports, and a host of other topics—is passed back and forth. Birth and adoptive parents get to know each other, and may even strike up a friendship. Some make plans to stay permanently in touch with one another, permitting the adoptee to maintain ties with his or her birth parents. Even in the most open adoption, however, the child's legal parents are the adoptive parents. Only they can make decisions about medical care, education, and other important matters.

Those who support open adoption are enthusiastic about what they see as its advantages. To begin with, they say, it is better for adoptees than are closed adoptions. There is no secrecy, so there is no need for lies or romantic tales, no playing As If. Adoptees are less likely to feel abandoned by their birth parents, especially when those parents stay in touch with the adoptive family. Health questions are easily answered.

Open adoption is better for birth parents, too, its supporters say. Birth parents who choose open adoption feel less of a sense of loss than parents who have to accept never seeing their child again. Just as important, they get to help choose the adoptive family. Today, using the Internet, birth parents can take an active part in selecting their child's adoptive family. They can choose parents who are black, white, Asian, or racially mixed, with or without other children, college educated or not—the list could go on and on.

Another benefit of open adoption is that it leaves a birth mother feeling more secure about the home in which her child is being raised. Birth mothers who have chosen closed adoption frequently report being haunted by fears that their children are being physically or emotionally abused. In an open adoption, birth parents may have an opportunity to monitor their child's welfare on a long-term basis.[23]

"I have a continually growing relationship with my son and his family," says one open-adoption birth mother. "I get to visit him a couple of times a year, which is wonderful. His mother . . . sends me . . . all sorts of wonderful things: pictures, letters, videotapes of the kids."[24]

Adoptive parents also can gain in open adoption, proponents say. They, as much as their adopted child, benefit from living without the burden of lies and evasions. They need not worry that a child who is unaware that he or she is adopted will somehow learn the truth and become angry or depressed as a result. They will have no reason to fear being hurt by a teenager or adult who suddenly announces the beginnings of a Search. And just as openness gives birth parents the opportunity to find just the kind of adoptive parents they want, it gives couples looking to adopt the chance to choose a birth mother. Adoptions in which the adoptive parents pick the birth mother are known as designated, or identified, adoptions.

One prominent supporter of adoption openness is Dave Thomas, founder of the Wendy's restaurant chain. Thomas was adopted at the age of six weeks, but was unaware of that fact until after his thirteenth birthday. Thomas describes himself as having been "really mad" when he learned that the truth had been kept from him. Today the Dave Thomas Center for Adoption Law sponsors programs aimed at promoting both open records and open adoption.[25]

But open adoption has its critics. Some feel that the practice is confusing for birth parents. Because an adoption is labeled "open," birth parents may not fully realize that they really are giving up their child to the adopting couple. Deep down, they may believe that they will continue to be important decision makers in the child's life.

Such a mistaken belief could mean future problems for the adoptive parents. What if a birth mother or father insists upon private school, rather than public, when the time comes? What if a birth parent demands visits from a child on birthdays or during holiday seasons? By law, the adoptive parents make the important decisions, but intrusive birth parents could seriously disrupt the life of an adoptive family. And what about the feelings of children caught between the wishes of their adoptive parents and the demands of their biological ones?

What if the relationship between birth and adoptive parents changes over time? Exchanges of photographs, letters, and visits may be frequent at first, then fall off. Birth parents may be more eager for contact than the adoptive parents are (and vice versa). On the other hand, birth parents may lose interest in the child as their lives fill up with new relationships and other children. How will the child react to any physical or emotional withdrawal?

What if the adoptive family moves to a different part of the country? Will contact with the birth family continue?

Other doubts center on the possibility that a birth mother's feelings about adoption will change during her pregnancy. A woman who has agreed in advance to relinquish her child to a couple she has met and come to like may change her mind after the baby arrives. If she decides to keep the child, it will be a cruel disappointment to the couple set to adopt. Perhaps the couple will urge the mother to live up to her agreement. If so, will she feel compelled to part with the newborn she now wants to parent? The pressure on the birth mother will be even more severe if the would-be adoptive parents have helped her with pregnancy-related expenses: medical bills, prenatal tests, housing. Such monetary assistance is customary in open and designated adoption.[26]

Or what if it's the couple planning to adopt that wants to back out of the deal? That could happen if, for example, the child to be adopted is born with some sort of a disability. Clearly, such issues need to be discussed, and alternative courses of action outlined, before the child is born.

The open adoption controversy and conflicts between privacy rights and the right of an adoptee to learn about his or her origins seem likely to continue into the future. So do disagreements about other adoption issues.

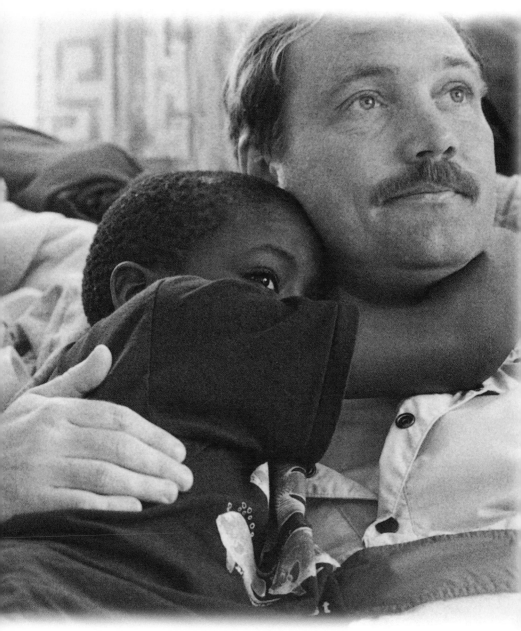

An interracial adoption

5
NONTRADITIONAL ADOPTIONS

Chuck and Penny adopted Tessa as an infant. The couple, who live in Maine, traveled to Chicago to pick up the baby, born to a single mother who had agreed to the adoption.

For seven years, Tessa lived as an only child. Then one day in 1999, Penny switched on the television news. Her attention was caught by a public service announcement. The announcement featured an eight-year-old girl named Vanessa.

Penny listened to Vanessa explain her situation. She was a foster child, she said, currently living in a temporary home. But she was eager to find a permanent family of her own. Was anyone out there interested? Penny recalls her reaction to Vanessa's appeal.

"There's Vanessa and she's saying, 'I love to sing and dance and I love pets and I'm outgoing,'" Penny later told a newspaper reporter. "I said, 'That's our daughter.'"

For some time Penny and Chuck had been contemplating adopting a second child. The moment they saw Vanessa—"It just clicked," Penny says. "We knew she was ours." Within weeks, social workers had placed Vanessa with the family. Adoption proceedings started.

Like her parents, Tessa is delighted with Vanessa. The girls have very different personalities—"like night and day"—Chuck says. Vanessa is strong and active and sometimes seems almost to overwhelm the quieter Tessa. Still, the two are learning what it means to be sisters. What is more, there is a special bond between them. Both are black. Chuck and Penny are white.[1]

Not long ago, such an adoption would have been unusual, and outright impossible in those states where racial prejudice had led to laws forbidding adoption or marriage between people of different races. Only in the 1970s were the last legal barriers to interracial adoption finally overturned. By that time adoption agencies were backing away from earlier policies that had called for the closest-possible matching of children with their adoptive parents.

Between 1958 and 1968, a U.S. government program arranged for the adoption of 395 Native American boys and girls by white families.[2] About

2,500 African-American children were placed with white parents in 1971.[3]

In the years since, the adoption of black children by white parents has become increasingly common largely due to a decline in the number of adoptable white infants. In the 1970s about 20 percent of unmarried white mothers agreed to relinquish their babies for adoption. Today, the percentage is down to less than 1.[4] Add to that statistic the fact that growing rates of infertility mean more and more white couples are turning to adoption, and it is easy to see why the number of interracial adoptive families is rising.[5] Yet interracial and transracial adoption—the latter generally refers to Asian or mixed-raced children going to white parents—remains controversial.

INTERRACIAL ADOPTION

Formal opposition to the adoption of black children by white couples initially surfaced during a 1972 meeting of the National Association of Black Social Workers (NABSW). "Black children should be placed only with black families, whether in foster care or adoption," the group declared in a resolution passed at that meeting.[6]

The resolution puzzles and dismays many white Americans. Penny, for one, cites her response to Vanessa's televised appeal, in which the girl specifically asked for parents who would help her learn about her racial background. Penny felt confident that she and Chuck could provide that help. Vanessa appears to be satisfied with their efforts. And Tessa is thrilled that her sister is black. "She looks just like me," Tessa told her mother excitedly the first time she met Vanessa.[7]

Why would the NABSW worry about the racial mix in Tessa and Vanessa's home? It's not as if plenty of children were not already growing up in racially diverse families. Marriages between members of various races—black, white, Native American, Hispanic, Asian, and so on—accounted for nearly 3 percent of all U.S. marriages in 1990.[8] The biological children of these marriages are being successfully raised in racially mixed homes.

As the NABSW sees it, though, an adoptive situation is different. Chuck and Penny can tell Vanessa and Tessa about the history of black Americans from the terrible days of slavery to the triumphs of great civil rights leaders like Dr. Martin Luther King Jr. They can find books about the land and people of Africa and read them with their daughters. They can help them celebrate Kwanza, the midwinter festival observed by many African Americans. But neither one can tell the children from personal experience what it means to be dark skinned in a society dominated by whites. Neither can share any deep knowledge of what life will be like for the girls as black adults or pass on to them strategies for handling racially motivated teasing or other problems. "Black children in white homes are cut off from the healthy development of themselves as black people," the NABSW contends. Lacking a genuine sense of what it means to be black will make it difficult for them to thrive in a society as race conscious as ours, the group insists.

The NABSW also has objected to the adoption of black youngsters by white couples on the grounds that it deprives the black community of some of its future citizens. As a statement of support for the 1972 resolution explains, ". . . we need our own to build a strong nation." Taking children out of African-American homes harms them as individuals while weakening as a group those who have been left behind.

A Form of Genocide? Most controversial of all, the 1972 resolution characterized interracial adoption as "a form of genocide." The dictionary defines genocide as "the systematic, planned annihilation of a racial, political, or cultural group." According to the United Nations (UN) genocide is ". . . the committing of certain acts with the intent to destroy—wholly or in part—a national, ethnic, racial or religious group as such, including . . . forcibly transferring children of one group to another."[9]

Of course no one is suggesting that Tessa and Vanessa's situation has anything to do with force—or genocide. So why is the word being used?

To answer that question we need to look back at history. The African-American experience is rooted in slavery. Slavery meant the buying and selling of human beings, and that meant the constant breakup of families. Married couples were split apart, babies torn from their parents' arms, children shipped off to new masters and mistresses far from home and family. This particular form of genocide, which African Americans endured for nearly 250 years, has left many with a special sensitivity to the issue.

Native Americans are also all too familiar with genocide. From the time Europeans first landed in America, whole tribes faced extermination by white people intent upon turning hallowed ancestral lands into profitable farms, ranches, and mines. Eventually, U.S. Army units were sent to confront the tribes and force them onto Indian reservations. By the late 1800s, government policies in both the United States and Canada dictated that Native American children be taken from their parents and sent to boarding schools. The idea was to improve the children's lives by teaching them to live and think like "civilized" white people. Actually, the schools were more like juvenile jails than educational facilities. Those forced into them were incarcerated for ten months of the year. Any who escaped were tracked down and locked up once more.[10]

Even after the boarding schools were shut down, the pattern of moving Native American children out of their own homes and into white ones persisted. In 1958 an agency of the U.S. government announced what it called the Indian Adoption Project. This was the program that resulted in the placing of 395 Native American children with white families over a ten-year period.[11]

At about the same time, Canada undertook a new removal program of its own. Thousands of native children were taken from their homes in British Columbia, Alberta, Ontario, and Manitoba and placed in nonnative foster or adoptive homes in other parts of the country. Some were sent as far away as the United States and Europe. The seizures reached peak numbers during the 1960s, earning them the label "Sixties Scoop." They did not end until the 1980s. By then the results had become devastatingly clear. Suicide, mental illness, drug and alcohol addiction—all were affecting the seized children and their biological families at exceptionally high rates. Following an investigation of the adoption program, one Canadian judge flatly denounced it as "cultural genocide."

Determined to change the way it treated its indigenous population, Canada introduced new policies intended to keep native children in their homes whenever possible.[12] In the United States, Native Americans threw their support behind the Indian Child Welfare Act of 1978. This law aims to slow—or stop—the outside adoption of Native American children and revive the tribes' ancient tradition of the kinship fostering of orphaned or abandoned children. Under the 1978 statute, anyone wishing to adopt a child with any blood ties to a Native American tribe must obtain the consent of both parents—and of the tribe itself. Some tribes are more willing than others to agree to an outside adoption.[13]

For its part, the NABSW has modified its stand on interracial adoption. The group's current position is that the adoption of black children by white couples is acceptable, but only as a last resort. Before any such adoption takes place, every effort should be made to reunite a child with his or her biological family or to arrange for adoption or fostering within the black community. In addition, the NABSW says, social workers should be less quick to remove black children from their biological homes and transfer them to foster care in the first place.[14]

In the recent past, social workers were indeed quick to take black children from their birth families. The number of black children in the U.S. foster care system went up by 50 percent between 1986 and 1991[15]—one reason for the kind of promotional campaign that introduced Vanessa to Chuck and Penny. Many black children in foster care are there because social workers believe they were abused or neglected in their own homes.

Removing a child from an abusive or neglectful home may sound like the only right course of action. However, the NABSW points out that abuse and neglect can usually be traced to poverty and the obstacles faced by single mothers, whose numbers are especially high among blacks.[16] As the group sees it, society should be doing more to fight poverty and assist single mothers to ensure that black families—and communities—stay together.

It is important to note, however, that many interracial and transracial adoptions do succeed. Aaron Moses Gooday-Ervin was a few weeks old when his birth parents, who were White Mountain Apaches, made up their minds to relinquish him for adoption. Those parents, in poor health and living in poverty, felt they had no other choice. Aaron's life changed dramatically. He went from living in a wickiup, a shelter made of sticks, surrounded by acres of empty land to a middle-class home in a Connecticut suburb. He adjusted, but never felt really comfortable there. "I just didn't fit in," he explains.

In his early twenties, Gooday-Ervin decided to seek out his roots. He returned to the reservation, where he learned that his birth parents were no longer living. He did, however, meet cousins. Those relatives greeted him joyously, telling him about his past—and his people's past. Today Gooday-Ervin combines his two worlds. He lives in Connecticut not far from his adoptive family, and near the Mashantucket Pequot Reservation. His wife is a Native American woman. Both work at the reservation and attend tribal events. "It's come full circle," says Gooday-Ervin's adoptive sister. "You can't replace knowing where you came from and having a connection to it."[17]

LOOKING ABROAD

Increasingly, couples unable to find adoptable children in the United States or Canada are looking overseas. The international adoption rate rose steadily from the 1950s through the 1990s. By 1996, adoptions from other countries were accounting for nearly a third of all U.S. adoptions of children under the age of two.[18]

Interest in international adoption is nothing new. It was, after all, an outpouring of public sympathy for those appealing World War I orphans from Belgium that spurred twentieth-century domestic adoption. Subsequent wars and disasters have left countless children homeless, and U.S. families have continued to respond.

After World War II, hundreds of children from Greece, Germany, Italy, and Japan were taken in by U.S. families. Thousands of the young victims of the Korean War (1950–53), in which U.S. and UN forces fought with South Korea against North Korea and China, also found new homes in America. American couples continued to adopt South Korean children for years after the war ended. Today there are about 100,000 Korean-American adoptees living in the United States. The Vietnam War (1950s–75), which pitted the United

States and South Vietnam against North Vietnam, similarly displaced large numbers of children and made many available for adoption.

Today, troubles in Eastern Europe are focusing attention there. For decades much of the area was dominated by the Soviet Union. Then in 1989, the Soviet Union began breaking up. Its disintegration meant freedom for a number of Eastern European nations.

For some of those nations, though, freedom brought with it civil war and economic chaos. Once again, the result was thousands of homeless children. In still other places—China, India, and Latin America, for example—poverty and social unrest have created millions more desperate youngsters. It is into such places that many preadoptive parents are venturing in search of children today. Highly visible international adoptions by celebrities such as actress Mia Farrow have helped draw public attention to the plight of needy children around the globe.

Still another reason for the surge in international and interracial adoption is that each offers a chance at parenthood for people who have traditionally been considered unsuitable as adoptive parents. Patricia Hluchy and Hamish Cameron of Toronto, Canada, for example, were eager to become parents. But Hluchy, who is unable to have children, would probably not have won approval to adopt a Canadian infant because at age forty-six, she would have been considered too old. So Hluchy and Cameron went to China, where age requirements are less restrictive. Writer Joan Oleck, who as a single woman knew she had "little chance" of adopting an infant in the United States, went to Russia, where the rules make it easier for singles to adopt. Oleck reports that two of her Manhattan neighbors, Margaret and Camilla, adopted a baby girl from China. Margaret and Camilla are lesbians.[19]

The Adoption Process How does international adoption work? After Hluchy and Cameron decided to adopt from China, their first step was to arrange for an adoption home study. Countries that allow foreigners to adopt their children demand the same thorough background checks as those needed in domestic adoptions.

Next, Hluchy and Cameron found an agency that specializes in international adoption—one of a growing number of such agencies in the United States and Canada. Like domestic adoptions, international adoptions must be processed through an accredited licensed agency. Workers at the agency Hluchy and Cameron chose helped the couple prepare their adoption dossier. This bulky file contained Hluchy's and Cameron's birth certificates, their marriage certificate, and medical, psychiatric, and police reports on each of them. It included proof of their financial ability to raise a child, personal recommendations, photographs of their home, and more.

The paperwork may have been daunting, but the adoption itself went quickly and easily. Hluchy and Cameron arrived in China on January 31, 1998. Within days they flew back to Canada with infant Zhi Flora Muriel Hluchy Cameron.[20] Compare that to the time it took Jacob and Michele Sullum to adopt Francine Allen. The relative ease and speed with which international adoptions can be completed is due to two factors. First, the children to be adopted have already been formally relinquished and are legally able to leave the country of their birth immediately. Second, the adoptive parents have completed all their paperwork and have been cleared to pick their children up soon after arrival. Ease and speed are two big reasons for the popularity of international adoption.

International adoption is not cheap, however. Legal and agency fees, travel expenses, and so on, can add up to $20,000 or more. This is considerably beyond what it typically costs to adopt domestically, although some domestic adoptions approach the $20,000 mark. In some cases questionable charges further inflate the cost of international adoption. Joan Oleck was ordered to hand over $11,000—in cash and without questions—to an orphanage worker in Russia before claiming her daughter Anya there in 1996.[21]

Triumphs and Troubles Most who have adopted children from other countries report being happy with the outcome. Retha and Roland Berube of Orrington, Maine, say their two Chinese-born daughters have adjusted perfectly to life in America. Anna, age five, loves soccer and Barbie dolls. Leia, three, favors Winnie the Pooh and pizza. The sisters could not be more American if they had been born at the local hospital, their parents say.[22] Legally, of course, they *are* Americans. Since 2001, federal legislation has conferred automatic U.S. citizenship on children adopted from overseas by Americans.

For some, international adoption becomes more than a mere family affair. In 1995, Brenda Baker and her husband Bob traveled to Latvia, a former Soviet nation, to adopt an eleven-month-old boy. Shortly thereafter, Baker returned for a seven-year-old girl. Two more Latvian adoptions followed, and in 1997, Baker founded a private group devoted to guiding other families through the complexities of adopting overseas.[23]

Although the actual adoptions are formalized through licensed adoption agencies, groups like Baker's can facilitate the process by helping prospective parents familiarize themselves with adoption laws and practices in the particular countries within which they are seeking children. Facilitators may also provide practical information about where parents might stay while the adoption is being finalized, what sort of clothing to bring along, the safety of the local water supply, and so on.

Anita Waxman is another who turned a simple adoption into something more. A single woman in her fifties, Waxman adopted Yuri from Russia when he was five years old. Until then, Yuri had lived in a Russian orphanage. Waxman describes the conditions there: "Kids are strapped to beds, dehydrated [from lack of fluids], and drugged to sleep." Eager to improve conditions for some of the country's young orphans, Waxman established a group home for abandoned children in Moscow.[24]

Unfortunately, not every international adoption story has a happy outcome. An Illinois couple, Steve and Polly Taber, adopted an eighteen-month-old Russian girl, Alina, in 1994. Six months later, they returned to Russia for four-year-old Alex.

The next two years were a nightmare for the Taber family. Alex, it turned out, had been so badly abused as a toddler that he was incapable of adjusting to normal family life. He continually kicked and pushed Alina. "He tried to stab her with scissors and me with a knife," his mother says. "He told us he'd burn the house down, he'd kill us. All this from a four year old."

No one involved in arranging Alex's adoption had told the Tabers the truth about his history of abuse. That sort of oversight—which sometimes amounts to outright deception—can happen in the confusion of adopting from overseas. The Tabers made mistakes, too. Papers documenting Alex's problems were handed over to them, but the couple did not bother having those documents translated from Russian into English.

"I feel sort of stupid," Steve Taber, a lawyer, told a reporter in 1996. He and his wife were on the verge of seeking another home for their son. They are not the only ones who have faced that sad decision. It's not known exactly how many adoptive families have relinquished a child for readoption, but experts say the number is growing. Several support groups for people like the Tabers have been formed. One has a membership of nine hundred families.

But by no means will every one of these families end up having to locate new homes for their children. Many will find that with time, love, and attention, the children will adjust.

Dr. Victor Groze of Case Western Reserve University in Ohio has studied nearly four hundred families who adopted children from the Eastern European nation of Romania, where orphanage conditions are as bad or worse than Anita Waxman saw in Russia. He discovered that badly damaged as many of the Romanian children were to begin with, most are now in surprisingly good shape. About 20 percent of them are actually thriving. "Resilient rascals," he calls this group. Another 60 percent are "wounded wonders," Groze says, children whose behavior has greatly improved, but who still lag behind others of their age. The remaining 20 percent are, like Alex Taber, terribly damaged.[25]

A Question of Heritage In most cases, the experience of families who adopt internationally falls somewhere between that of the Tabers and that of people like the Bakers or the Berubes. Most find that although relationships generally work out, adjustment can be rocky at times.

As a young child, Kim, adopted from Vietnam by a U.S. family, was attracted by the children with Asian features she sometimes saw when her mother took her shopping. She used to follow those children around the supermarket staring at their faces. When she reached her teens Kim repeatedly told her parents that she planned to return to Vietnam to marry. That way, she said, she would at least have children who looked like her.[26] Elizabeth Bartholet is the adoptive mother of two boys from Peru. Many Peruvians are dark skinned, evidence of their Inca heritage. When her younger son was three, Bartholet says, he told her that he wanted her to look more like him. "I wish you were the same color," he said wistfully.[27]

Race is only one issue when it comes to international adoption. Culture and religion can be major concerns as well.

Stephen Chen is one parent who wants to be sure his daughter Lindsay, adopted from China, grows up with an awareness of her cultural background. The four year old is learning the Chinese language and studying Chinese art and calligraphy. For Chen, it is easy to provide Lindsay with such rich cultural opportunities. He lives in Boston, home to a large and active Chinese community. It may be harder for the Berubes to provide authentic Chinese experiences for Anna and Leia in largely white rural Maine.

Of course, not all parents want to educate their internationally adopted children about the culture they left behind. Some are convinced the children will be better off the more deeply they become part of American culture. They may be right. On the other hand, is it fair to bring children up ignorant of the traditions that helped form them?

Finally, there is the matter of religion. Many who adopt have a strong religious faith. Understandably, they want their children to share their faith. That may mean taking someone from a Buddhist, Hindu, or other religious background and bringing him or her up as a Catholic, Protestant, or Jew. How are children going to feel later on when they realize that they have unknowingly been converted from one religion to another? How will they react as they mature into adolescents and adults?

How will they deal with other cultural and racial distinctions between themselves and their adoptive parents? What will happen if they, like so many adoptees before them, decide they want to learn something about their birth families? Will they ever be able to initiate a Search? Some of the questions are troubling, but it is encouraging to remember that most of the children adopted earlier in the twentieth century from places like Europe and Korea have adapted well to life in America.[28]

Thomas Masters is one who adapted successfully. Born in Korea in the mid-1950s as Suh Ung Ki, he was adopted by an American couple when he was five years old. He and his sister, also adopted from Korea, grew up in Wichita, Kansas. Tommy, as he was called, soon forgot anything he had ever known about Korea—its language, its food, its culture. He forgot the names of his biological siblings, almost forgot, he says today, that he was Korean at all. Only when Tommy and his sister were teased by other children did the fact of their "Koreanness" come home to them.

As an adult, Masters became a police officer, then went to law school and joined the Federal Bureau of Investigation (FBI). It was as an FBI agent that he first came in contact with a Korean-American organization. It was a revelation. Talking with older Korean-Americans made him realize that his heritage was unique. "As far as I was concerned, Korea, Japan, China—those areas were all the same," Masters says of his earlier attitude. Today he relishes Korea's distinctive history and culture. He uses his new understanding to help U.S. parents who have adopted internationally find ways to educate their children about their cultural roots.[29]

Embracing Differences Today's international and interracial adoptees and their families have an advantage over their counterparts of a few years ago: There are so many more of them. Just about any adoptive family wrestling with issues of religion, culture, and race can find other families who share similar concerns. And these families have a variety of resources available to them. A quick check of the Internet will turn up hundreds of informative books and articles. The Internet may also lead families to adoption chat rooms and support groups—and to places like the East India Colorado Heritage Camp.

Heritage camps like this one began appearing in the 1980s to serve children adopted from Korea. Today they are also open to children from Vietnam, India, Latin America, the Philippines, and many other nations.

Gina Gruelle, age nineteen, speaks enthusiastically about Heritage Camp. Gina was born in India and grew up in a small Oregon town where she never saw another person who looked like her. At Heritage Camp, she was surrounded by people with features and skin color like her own. Now a counselor at the camp, Gina points out, "It's important to go someplace where people do look and feel like you."

Colorado's Heritage Camp is not unique. At a Maine camp for families with children adopted from China, children enjoy regular camp activities with a cultural twist—preparing Chinese food, learning Chinese songs and dances—while their parents take part in discussions about what it's like to live in a mixed-race family or how to deal with their children's cultural needs and questions. This camp was founded by the Boston chapter of Families with Children from China, an international adoption support group.[30] Like Heritage Camp, and like all the other camps, groups, and services available to international and interracial families, it helps families understand and appreciate their differences.

GAY AND LESBIAN ADOPTION

Of all those who face barriers to becoming adoptive parents, homosexuals probably face the toughest barriers of all. It is virtually impossible for gays or lesbians, whether as single individuals or together as partners, to adopt a healthy infant in this country. Only if a homosexual agrees to take a hard-to-place special-needs child—an adolescent, for instance, or a child who is physically, mentally, or emotionally disabled—does he or she have much chance of winning agency approval as an adoptive parent. Independent adoption is also difficult for homosexuals, since birth parents generally prefer a child to go to a married couple. No wonder more and more gays and lesbians are looking to adopt abroad—in countries where requirements are less stringent.

But should homosexuals be allowed to adopt at all? That's where the debate begins.

"Under no circumstances should a child be allowed to be brought up in a homosexual environment," says the Reverend Maurice Gordon, a pastor in a Pentecostal church in Denver, Colorado. Like a number of other religious conservatives, Catholic, Protestant, and Jewish, Gordon believes that homosexuality is morally wrong. That is reason enough all by itself, he and others assert, to keep children from being adopted into gay and lesbian homes.

Gordon also expresses the fear that children living in homosexual homes are at risk of sexual abuse. Although he concedes that a child adopted by a homosexual might not "automatically" be molested by his or her parent, the threat is still there. "[H]e probably would be abused by the homosexual's friends," Gordon says.

However, experts at the Child Welfare League of America and others dismiss Gordon's assumption as unfounded. Abuse in a homosexual adoptive home is no more likely than abuse in any other adoptive home, the league maintains. Its figures show that 90 percent of those who sexually abuse children are heterosexual men.[31]

But there are other concerns as well, say those who oppose gay adoption. Some believe that children raised by gays or lesbians will develop psychological problems or that they will grow up to be gay or lesbian themselves. Others worry that children with two mothers or two fathers will be teased or harassed by their classmates.

Abby Ruder, a therapist, lesbian, and adoptive mother, admits that teasing is inevitable. She adds, though, that just as any parents try to prepare a child for being teased—about wearing glasses, for instance, or being overweight—so too can homosexual parents. With careful planning, Ruder says, homosexuals can help their children deal with any taunts that come their way. "Children with gay or lesbian parents need to be taught when it's okay to tell people and when not to," she advises. "My nine year old . . . has become very adept at knowing when to tell people that she has two mommies." It helps, too, if children adopted by homosexuals live in cities like New York or San Francisco, with their sizable gay populations. They will almost certainly find more support and understanding there than they would in a small town in a more conservative part of the country.

Julie, who was raised in a lesbian household, agrees that teasing is going to occur. "There were times when I felt embarrassed," she acknowledges. "But when I think about my growing up years, I was happier than most of my friends." Julie, now in her early twenties, does not believe that she suffered any psychological damage as a result of having two mothers. "I feel good about who I am," she says. Julie and Abby Ruder's daughter are just two of the many children who were being raised in homosexual households in the United States in the 1990s.

As for the concern that the children of homosexuals will naturally grow up to be homosexual, most researchers dismiss the idea. Some may be homosexual, just as some of the children of heterosexuals are. But according to the National Adoption Information Clearinghouse (NAIC), which operates through the U.S. Department of Health and Human Services, the bulk of evidence indicates that children raised by homosexuals are no more likely to be gay or lesbian than those raised by heterosexuals.

New Recommendations In 1998, after weighing the evidence, the Child Welfare League recommended an end to discrimination against gays and lesbians as adoptive parents. The group called for social workers to assess gay and lesbian applicants for adoptive parenthood just as they would assess any other applicants. The North American Council on Adoptable Children (NACAC), which operates throughout the United States and Canada, has made a similar recommendation. According to NACAC policy, "Everyone with the potential to successfully parent a child . . . is entitled to fair and equal consideration regardless of sexual orientation or differing lifestyle. . . . "[32]

Homosexuals and those who support the right of homosexuals to adopt are encouraged by the recommendations. They know, however, that given the combination of antigay prejudice and the shortage of healthy adoptable U.S. infants, the reality is that for homosexuals, adoption will continue to center on international and special-needs children.

Yet another issue for gay and lesbian parents involves what is known as second-parent, or coparent, adoption.

For heterosexual couples, second-parent adoption is nothing new. Suppose Jimmy's mother has died. If Jimmy's father remarries, he may ask his new wife not just to act as Jimmy's mother but to take the legal steps necessary to adopt the boy formally. That way, if he dies, Jimmy will still have a legal parent—and a permanent home of his own. If one of Jimmy's parents had been divorced, or was previously unmarried, he or she might also ask a new spouse to apply for second-parent adoption. Of course no such adoption can occur unless the second birth parent is dead or has agreed to relinquish the child.

When it comes to homosexuals, second-parent adoption is not so easy. Take Margaret and Camilla, the lesbian couple who adopted their daughter Miranda in China.

Actually, the couple did not adopt Miranda. Camilla did. Chinese law does not allow homosexuals to adopt, so Camilla filed papers as a single woman.[33]

That left Margaret with no legal relationship to Miranda. And since New York is one of the thirty-nine states that refuses to allow second-parent adoption by a homosexual's same-sex partner, Margaret cannot win such a relationship with the little girl.[34] If something happens to Camilla, Margaret will have no legal right to the child she regards as her own daughter. It is conceivable that Miranda could be taken from Margaret and put into New York foster care.

That would be sad indeed, believe gay adoption supporters. As Joan Oleck says—with Miranda in mind—". . . two moms, or even one for that matter, are ever so much better than none."[35]

6
QUESTIONS AND CONTROVERSIES

Adoption sounds as if it should be simple. A woman gives birth to a child that she cannot, for one reason or another, care for as a parent. She relinquishes her legal right to the child, giving it up for adoption either independently or through an agency. A couple waiting to adopt learns that a baby is available. After taking all the necessary steps and having been thoroughly reviewed, the couple takes the child home. Everyone lives happily ever after.

But adoption is not simple. We've already looked at some of the controversies that complicate it: the long drawn-out process, the issue of secrecy versus openness, debates over who is fit to adopt,

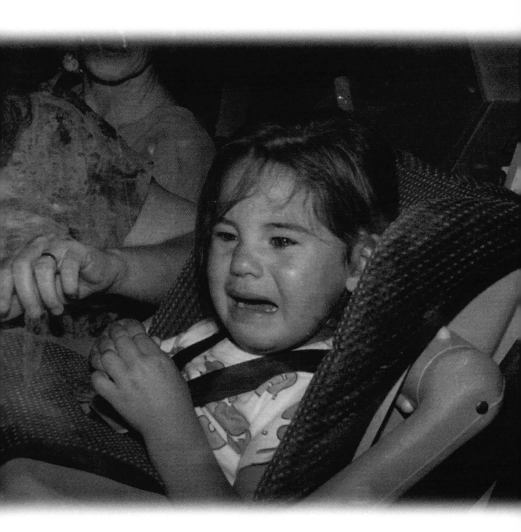

Baby Jessica,
a controversial case

uncertainty about the best ways of handling delicate matters of race and culture, and so on. There are other complex adoption issues as well.

PERMANENCY

Once, most people assumed that adoptions could not be undone. Then they began hearing about the Baby Jessica case.

The case began with a newborn adopted in 1991 by a Michigan couple—Jan and Roberta DeBoer. The DeBoers wanted to adopt independently, but since Michigan did not allow independent adoption at the time, they decided to look out of state. Eventually they located an unmarried Iowa birth mother, Cara Clausen, who agreed to an adoption plan.

The fact that two separate states were involved meant that in adopting, the DeBoers would have to follow the guidelines set forth in the Interstate Compact on the Placement of Children (ICPC), a law that comes into play when an adoption between a child and non-related adults involves moving the child from one state to another. All fifty states, the District of Columbia, and the U.S. Virgin Islands abide by the ICPC in order to safeguard children by making sure that the state into which they are adopted offers them the same protections and services they would receive in their birth state.

The ICPC presented no obstacle to the DeBoers. Adoption proceedings began. The couple named their new daughter Jessica.

But for the DeBoers, there was to be no "happily ever after." Shortly after the adoptive parents took their baby home, problems surfaced. In 1993, after a long legal battle and amid a blaze of publicity, the

Supreme Court of the state of Iowa ruled that the DeBoers must give up the child they had raised and loved for two and a half years. By order of the court, Jessica was taken from the only mother and father she had known and returned to her birth family in Iowa. Pictures of Jessica—strapped into a child car seat and sobbing pitifully—horrified the nation. Few Americans had realized that such an adoption tragedy was possible.

The reaction was especially strong among adoptive parents. Many panicked, terrified that the children they had adopted years before would suddenly be snatched away by birth relatives they had never known or almost forgotten. Feeding adoptive parents' fears were news reports about other birth parents who had relinquished children and were now declaring their intentions of going to court to get them back. Even today, the mere thought of the Baby Jessica decision is enough to send some adoptive parents into a tailspin. The case is just one more reason for the growing popularity of international adoption. Some adoptive parents figure it's unlikely that birth parents in places like Russia or Peru will decide to travel to the United States and try to reclaim their children.

But according to adoption law experts, the fear and unease were—are—largely unfounded. Out of the thousands of adoptions that take place in the United States each year, only "a handful" are challenged in court, says adoption attorney Stanton Phillips. And, he adds, "most of those end favorably for the adoptive family."

What is more, the Iowa ruling does *not* mean that birth parents can casually change their minds and regain custody of a legally adopted child. It *does* mean that adoptive parents like the DeBoers need to keep a close eye on every aspect of an adoption proceeding and make sure they understand their rights—and the rights of the birth parents.

The DeBoers knew almost from the start that there were problems with the adoption. Cara Clausen, it turned out, had not told her former boyfriend, Dan Schmidt, that he was her baby's father. Furthermore, in supplying information for the baby's birth certificate, Clausen had lied. Instead of naming Schmidt as the father, Clausen gave the name of her then-fiance. As a result, Schmidt never had the opportunity to sign—or refuse to sign— formal relinquishment papers.

Jessica had been with the DeBoers for only a few weeks when Clausen confessed the truth to Schmidt. Schmidt immediately went to court to claim his daughter. Clausen joined him, hoping to regain custody herself.

Clausen's case was based on her contention that the DeBoers' lawyer had failed to give her enough time to think about her decision to relinquish her parental rights. She maintained that she had been persuaded to sign relinquishment papers sooner than was required under Iowa adoption law. By the time Clausen changed her mind, the baby was already with the DeBoers.

Even though Schmidt had a strong case, the DeBoers chose to fight him and Clausen every step of the way. The legal battle dragged on for over two years, years during which—as many see it—the best interests of a child were overridden by a conflict between two sets of parents, each determined to get its own way. In the end Schmidt won custody of Jessica on the grounds that his rights as a father had been violated. Clausen did not regain legal parenthood.[1] Today, Jessica—now Anna Schmidt—lives mostly with her father.[2] Her adoption was not undone. It had never been complete.

Adoptive parents can take further comfort from a 1995 California adoption case. In this instance, the court ruled against a birth father who was trying to block his son's adoption. The reasoning behind the ruling: The father had not previously taken an active part in the child's life.

To win custody, the California court said, a father must show interest in a child "within a short time after he learned or reasonably should have learned that the biological mother was pregnant with his child." The California father, who had broken up with his son's mother and ignored the child for months, had not met that standard, the court decided. Dan Schmidt, who acted as soon as he learned he had a daughter, had. A birth father who refuses to support his child's mother during her pregnancy or who fails to show an interest in the child after he or she is born is unlikely to win custody. Adoptive couples can hope that rulings like the one in California are repeated in other states, since at least half of all adoptions are finalized without the birth father's consent. In most instances, consent is lacking because the father cannot be located.[3]

Efforts to correct this situation, and to involve birth fathers more fully in their children's lives, are underway across the country. In many states, birth fathers are now required to submit their names to a birth father registry, or otherwise identify themselves as the father of a particular infant. (Of course, birth fathers who want nothing more to do with the birth mother, or who are determined not to have to help care for or provide for a child, will often find ways of avoiding registration.) Theoretically, adoption agencies are responsible for locating birth fathers and getting them to sign relinquishment papers, but this is not always possible. In addition, laws regarding the rights of birth fathers vary widely from state to state. In some, fathers are allowed to relinquish their parental claims at, or even before, the time of a child's birth. In others, they may have weeks—or months after the child is born to make up their minds about adoption.[4]

BABY-SELLING

Baby-selling stories appear with depressing regularity in the news media and are of concern to people looking to adopt as well as to those involved with children's welfare.

In April 2000, a New York woman was accused of offering her unborn child to a couple in return for over $1,000. State officials stepped in, and after the child was born, placed the child in foster care.[5] A year earlier, a lawyer, also from New York, advertised on the Internet for a couple willing to pay $60,000 for a ten-week-old infant. The lawyer was working in league with the child's mother, a Hungarian woman living in the United States. Authorities described the two as "trafficking in human life." In this instance, too, the baby went into foster care.[6] All three would-be baby-sellers were charged with criminal wrongdoing.

It goes without saying that black-market adoption is against the law in every state and throughout Canada. But what is it exactly?

To some, baby-selling occurs any time there is any connection whatsoever between money and adoption. Adoption is about building loving families, these people protest. Money should never be involved.

That may be a high-minded attitude—but it is also an unrealistic one. Paying for legitimate adoption costs is not the same as paying for a baby. Adoption agencies have to charge potential adopters for the services they offer. It costs an agency money to provide basic information about adoption, process applications, conduct and evaluate home studies, and the like.

The distinction between paying for services and paying for a child is a useful one and in domestic adoption, it is usually easy enough to tell the two apart. For a couple adopting independently, it is routine to cover a birth mother's medical and living expenses. A couple may also pay the mother's share of whatever a facilitator or intermediary charges and reimburse the lawyer who helps her complete the adoption. Such payments are entirely legal. For a couple to offer to pay a birth mother's college or vocational school tuition, however, is not. Nor is it permissible for them to take her shopping at the mall or send her off on a Disneyland vacation. Such "extras" have nothing to do with the birth or adoption of a baby. The courts would regard them as payment for a child and put a quick end to the couple's adoption hopes.[7] By the same token, paying a lawyer for the legal services he or she provides in finalizing the adoption is acceptable. Paying him or her to locate a baby and pass it along is not.

One intriguing aspect of the 1999 New York baby-selling incident is the fact that the lawyer involved used the Internet to advance his scheme. Use of the Internet troubles some people. Bill Pierce, president of the National Council for Adoption in Washington, DC, is one who believes that a new era of cyberspace adoption crime looms on the horizon.

Going online to find adoptable children "is very dangerous," Pierce warns preadoptive parents. "All the Internet does is to make it easier for people to perpetrate [baby-selling] scams." But those who see the Internet as a valuable resource for locating adoptable children dismiss Pierce's warning. They point out that lawyers and other professionals will be brought into the case long before any adoption is finalized. Their presence will serve to protect the interests of adoptive parents and lessen the likelihood of fraud. It also helps safeguard children in danger of being victimized in any baby-selling scheme.[8] One Internet expert in England reminds people that it is relatively easy to follow transactions that take place in cyberspace. "The Net is trackable," he says. It may actually be easier to catch baby-sellers online than off.[9]

INTERNATIONAL BLACK-MARKET ADOPTION

When it comes to international adoption, the distinction between paying for services and paying for a child can get blurry.

Like domestic adoption, international adoption is a complex procedure. That's why Brenda Baker and others familiar with the process are committed to helping first-time adoptive parents work with agency officials at home and abroad as they complete the adoption process.

But even with help, those who choose international adoption may find themselves bewildered by its intricacies. There are government forms to fill out, some required by the receiving country (into which the child is to be adopted), others by the sending country (where the child was born). Each completed form must be returned with a separate processing fee. Adopting parents may be given documents written in languages they do not understand. If that happens, they may want to hire translators. Intermediaries, facilitators, and agencies may charge their own fees. Adopting parents are apt to feel they are handing out money left and right. Is it all going for services? How can they—tired from travel, isolated in a hotel room in a strange country, apprehensive about their child's health and well-being, surrounded by people they have never met before, not knowing the language—be sure?

Joan Oleck had no doubt that something was amiss when a worker at the Russian orphanage from which she was adopting her daughter Anya demanded $11,000 in cash. This was no fee for service. If Oleck wanted to take Anya back to the United States, she would have to pay up.

What should she do? Forking over the money would make Oleck part of a despicable black-market operation. But at the same time, she was eager to get Anya, whom she already loved, home. Looking around the orphanage, Oleck knew her mind was made up. "Staffers were too busy to do much more than attend to the children's most basic daily needs," she says. "So babies stood in their cribs with arms outstretched, begging to be held. Or they rocked on their knees endlessly, looking for love and unable to find it." Oleck paid. Did she make the right choice?

The ethics of Oleck's decision aside, the international baby-selling business does go on. Bribery is not uncommon in adoptions from countries in Latin America and Eastern Europe, Oleck says. In Russia, some penniless women feed themselves and their older children by "selling their newborns to the highest Western bidders."

Some Americans are also profiting financially from the international adoption black market. Two Long Island, New York, women were arrested in May 1999 and charged with illegally smuggling Mexican infants into the United States and selling them to couples desperate to adopt.[10] In another type of scam, an agency called Today's Adoption bilked scores of hopeful couples out of a total of $285,000 between 1990 and 1996. The black-market agency promised the couples babies from Paraguay, Chile, and other countries—but never delivered. One heartbroken couple lost $15,000. Another lost $30,000. "Adoption hell," is how one man described his dealings with Today's Adoption. In 1996, New York state officials shut the agency down in that state.[11]

THE HAGUE CONVENTION

Can anything be done to stop the corruption? Action is already under way. On May 29, 1993, negotiators meeting at The Hague, capital of the Netherlands, agreed to the Hague Convention on

Protection of Children and Co-operation in Respect of Intercountry Adoption.

The Hague Convention can be likened to an international version of the Interstate Compact on the Placement of Children. It is designed to bring about an end to the international baby-selling business and to safeguard the interests of all the parties concerned in international adoption—children, birth parents, adoptive parents, even nations themselves. The United States signed the treaty in 1994, one of forty countries to have done so by mid-2000.

But the treaty does not go into effect until the countries ratify it.[12] U.S. ratification occurred on September 20, 2000, when the Senate, the upper house of the U.S. Congress, voted in favor of the treaty. Just over two weeks later, President Bill Clinton signed the "Intercountry Adoption Act of 2000" into law.

The Hague Convention will be a boon to many Americans seeking to adopt internationally. The treaty sets strict standards for sending nations like Russia and China. A sending nation must provide clear proof that a child is adoptable—unlike little Alex Taber, whose sad history we looked at in chapter five. Adoption workers in the sending country must also investigate each potential adoptee's circumstances in order to be sure that adoption is in his or her best interests. They must see to it that the birth parents have relinquished their child voluntarily, fully understanding what they were committing themselves to. Black-market payoffs will not be permitted.

The treaty offers guarantees to sending nations as well. International adoption agencies in receiving countries must offer evidence that the adopting parents are fit and eligible to adopt, that they understand the adoption process, and that the child will be allowed to live permanently in his or her new country.[13]

Above all, the Hague Convention, if ratified worldwide, will help children by allowing more of them than ever before to find safe and loving homes.

It is beyond question that millions of children desperately need such homes. According to Anthony D'Amato, a law professor at Northwestern University, there are an estimated 40 million homeless children scrounging a living on city streets in Latin America alone.[14] Russia reported 113,000 orphaned or abandoned newborns in 1997 and another 113,000 the next year.[15] Thirteen million African children had been orphaned or half-orphaned by the end of 2000 as a result of AIDS, Acquired Immune Deficiency Syndrome. AIDS has reached epidemic proportions in southern and central Africa.[16] Around the globe, as many as 250 million children under the age of fourteen are working to support themselves or their families, many in slavery or near-slavery.[17] The figures are staggering and the need obvious.

Yet as it stands now, many nations, including some of the world's poorest, are reluctant to allow their children to be adopted outside the land of their birth.

When Brenda Baker and her husband adopted their first child from Latvia, a Latvian judge asked them whether they wanted the boy so they could sell his organs—liver, kidneys, and so on—to save the lives of American children. Baker was dumb-founded by the suggestion, which seemed "ridiculous" to her.[18] But the fears of a sending nation cannot be easily dismissed. People in some countries worry that their children will be "treated as servants or otherwise misused," says Maureen Evans, executive director of the Joint Council on International Children's Services, an umbrella group of international adoption agencies.[19] After all, it wasn't so many years ago that destitute or orphaned children in Western Europe and America were bound out as indentured servants, shipped away to unknown destinations, forced into dangerous, even deadly, jobs. International misgivings are understandable.

Another reason a nation may hesitate to permit the international adoption of its children is that government officials sometimes face criticism for allowing rich outsiders to descend upon their country and raid its orphanages. After domination by the Soviet Union ended in Romania late in 1989, says Anthony D'Amato, Americans and others began adopting children out of that country's state-run orphanages. "The Romanian press criticized the government for 'exporting our precious human capital' and for selling 'our birthright to greedy, wealthy foreigners,'" D'Amato wrote in *Christian Century* magazine. The government's response was to put an end to the adoptions until such time as they would be able to establish a system of regulations and protocol to process adoptions properly.[20] In May 2000 the Russian government considered limiting international adoptions from that country after hearing complaints that Americans were shopping for children in Russia "as if they were going to Wal-Mart."[21] If the Hague Convention is ratified by the world's major receiving countries, the safeguards it puts in place should leave government authorities in sending countries less vulnerable to such criticisms.

THE CRISIS IN FOSTER CARE

In 1997 there were approximately half a million children in foster care across the United States. That was up from just over 400,000 in 1990. Exact figures are hard to pin down, partly because statistics are collected on a city-by-city, state-by-state basis. In addition, there is sometimes a question of who is in foster care and who is not. Before the late 1980s, New York City children who were being cared for by relatives other than parents were not counted as foster children. After 1990, they were.

More disturbing than the size of the foster-child population is the length of time many children spend as part of that population. Of the 35,000-odd children in foster care in New York City in 1998, fewer than 4,000 were adopted—and that only after each had spent an average of nearly seven years living in various temporary homes.[22]

Seven years! In seven years an infant becomes a first grader. Seven more and that first grader is a teenager. Another seven and she is a legal adult. Is a system that compels a child to spend one-third of her childhood and adolescence being shifted around from one family to another to another being fair to that child?

"Time counts for foster children," says Robert Schwartz, executive director of the Juvenile Law

Center in Philadelphia. "The price of delay for children is a hidden scandal."[23]

Why the delay in getting foster children into permanent homes? The question has several answers. One problem is that competent adoption social workers are in short supply. The shortage means that each social worker has more cases than he or she can handle efficiently. Another is that law courts are jammed with cases waiting to be heard. Even when a child's case does finally come before a judge, that judge may not be the same one who heard the same child's case in earlier stages. The new judge will need extra time to become familiar with the facts of the case, which leads to another delay.

There are also delays while paperwork is completed. Computers would speed the process, but in the foster care field access to computers is limited. "In some jurisdictions it's still file folders in drawers," says a spokesman for the U.S. Department of Health and Human Services. "If the social worker isn't in, there's no information available and the child's case can't move forward."

Other reasons for delay include the limited number of families willing to become foster parents, especially to children with special needs. Some social workers won't even try to place a disabled youngster. But perhaps the most important reason of all for delay is that judges and others in the adoption field are reluctant to legally and permanently break the ties between children and their blood kin.

Cornilous Pixley was three months old in 1996 when his mother, Latrena Pixley, went to jail for killing her five-week-old daughter four years earlier. Cornilous was put into the care of a foster mother,

Laura Blankman, a police officer in Maryland. Three years later, Cornilous had become what one magazine writer called "the poster child for what's wrong with the way courts handle kids."

Laura Blankman applied to adopt Cornilous. But before the process really got going, Latrena Pixley was released from jail. Pixley immediately went to court to try to regain custody of her son. In December 1997 a judge ordered Blankman to turn Cornilous over to his biological mother.

"Why would a judge take a small child from a cop and give him to a murderer?" the magazine writer asked. Simple, says Bob Tuke of the American Academy of Adoption Attorneys. U.S. laws tend to emulate (copy) old English laws. English law has traditionally emphasized the over-riding importance of blood ties. In the case of Cornilous Pixley, ancient attitudes about preserving the biological family may have been reenforced by modern ideas about race. Cornilous is black. Blankman is white.

Blankman appealed the judge's decision. First one court heard her appeal, then another. Neither came to a decision. At age three and a half, Cornilous's future was still in doubt.[24]

Changes in the Law In 1997, Congress passed and President Bill Clinton signed into law the Adoption and Safe Families Act. This law is intended to increase adoption rates among children in foster care. It authorizes the federal government to pay cash bonuses to states that succeed in raising the number of foster children placed in permanent adoptive homes. For each child placed, a state gets

$4,000. If the adoptee is considered to be a special-needs child, that figure jumps to $6,000.[25] Federal officials expect the states to use their bonus money to hire more, and better qualified, social workers to streamline the adoption process. The payments were set to begin in 1999 and will run through 2003.

Another federal law offers adoption incentives directly to families. Under the Small Business Job Protection Act, effective as of January 1, 1997, a family that adopts a child gets a break on its tax bill. The family is allowed to keep $5,000 of what it would normally owe in federal income tax for the year in which the adoption occurs. Adoptions involving U.S.-born special-needs children earn families a $6,000 tax break.[26]

Will tax incentives, combined with bonuses to states that raise adoption rates, help get children out of foster care and into homes of their own? Adoption professionals hope so. As they see it, the country's foster care system as it exists today is in crisis.

Good News—and Bad The good news is that adoptions of foster children are up. Between 1996 and 1998—the year before the new laws were enacted or took effect—adoptions of foster children rose from 28,000 to 36,000, an increase of almost 30 percent. Adoption rates rose in thirty-five states. The state with the greatest gain was Hawaii where adoptions rose by 249 percent. The lowest gains—2 percent each—were in Massachusetts and New York. The states that showed improvement received their first Adoption and Safe Families Act bonus awards at a September 1999 White House ceremony hosted by President Clinton.[27]

Even in New York, with its small 2 percent gain, there was good news. The number of foster children in that state reached its lowest level in a decade. In 1991, the state had counted 49,100 children in foster care, compared to 35,200 in 1999. But while city officials were pleased by the decline in numbers, critics pointed out that much of the drop was due to children reaching the age of eighteen and leaving the system. Worse, the critics said, New York foster children who were adopted were still waiting the same long years for permanent homes. The Adoption and Safe Families Act goal is to make children available for adoption as soon as they have spent fifteen of the most recent twenty-two months in foster care. In one-third of cases, a study found, New York City foster care officials were not even making an attempt to meet that goal.[28]

Others were skeptical about the chances that measures like the Adoption and Safe Family Act will mean genuine improvement in the lives of foster children. In Tennessee a children's advocacy group brought suit, charging that state foster care officials were blatantly ignoring federal law. Tennessee children removed from their families because of abuse or neglect were not being made available for adoption, the group said. Some were kept in emergency shelters for months at a time. About 2,000 had been moved into and out of ten or more different foster homes during their short lives.[29]

Even simple technological improvements are slow in coming. In New York a computer system, ordered in 1995 to lighten the paperwork load and accelerate the foster-care-to-adoption process, was still not in place five years later. As of mid-2000, the $200 million-plus system could not so much as tell a social worker where any one particular foster child was living.[30]

Lost in Foster Care Sloppy record keeping does more than delay adoption. It can keep children from being reunited with biological families that may be capable of caring for them. In New York City, the records of some foster children contain no information about the steps biological parents must take if they want to regain custody. Such steps might include starting treatment for drug or alcohol problems or attending parenting classes. In a number of cases, it was not clear whether social workers had bothered to tell parents what they needed to do to get their children back.[31]

In extreme cases, records are so haphazard that, from a parent's point of view, children in foster care appear to vanish altogether. That was the experience of a New York man identified only as Mr. H.

Mr. H., a limousine driver, was living with his wife and their two children, Dawn, age four, and Daniel, three, when Mrs. H. left him, taking the children with her. Two or three years later, in 1991, city authorities found the children alone, malnourished, and probably abused, in their mother's apartment. Daniel and Dawn were placed in foster care.

Meanwhile, Mr. H. had been desperately searching for his children. He put up missing children posters, hired a private detective, and combed city neighborhoods on his own. The year 1991 came and went and Mr. H., unaware that Daniel and Dawn were in foster care, continued his search. Not until 1994, when city social workers decided to release the children for adoption, did foster care officials begin trying to locate their father. The three were reunited, but it was too late for them as a family. The children had no memory of their father. Dawn rebelled and ran away from home when she was seventeen. Daniel had a mental breakdown. Mr. H., and four other men with foster care horror stories that resemble his, have brought lawsuits against the city.[32]

"Aging Out" Finally, there is the troubling issue of what happens to foster children when they become adults. Foster children generally "age out" of the system on their eighteenth birthdays, although some may continue to live in group foster homes or receive other forms of assistance until they have reached twenty-one.

At whatever age they leave, their overall prospects are not bright. "All the research suggests that this is a group at high risk of incarceration, homelessness, public assistance, dependency, out-of-wedlock childbearing and victimization—being sexually and physically victimized," says Mark E. Courtney. Courtney, a professor of social work at the University of Wisconsin, is one of the few researchers who have conducted a large-scale study of post-foster care children. His assessment makes for gloomy reading.

Courtney's study showed that 25 percent of young men are in prison within twelve to eighteen months of leaving foster care. Among former foster care girls, one in ten is raped during the same time span. One-third of those leaving the system have not finished high school and fewer than one-fifth have received any job training. While these discouraging statistics may owe something to the physical, mental, and emotional disabilities that affect so many foster children, they also have much to do with the disruptions the youngsters faced throughout childhood. And they sound a warning about the foster-care system as it exists in much of the country today. Any family that turned out such a high rate of criminals, victims, and people lacking in life skills would be considered severely dysfunctional. "When we presume to do better than their parents and do in fact replace their parents," Courtney says, "then we have to look critically at what we as parents are responsible for."

Yet in a few instances society meets its foster care responsibilities very well. Quantwilla Johnson spent fifteen years in New York City's foster-care system. In the spring of 2000 she was a twenty-year-old college student, studying communications at a branch of the State University of New York. Quantwilla, only three when she entered foster care, was lucky—she was placed in a loving foster home and was never moved from that home. Speaking of the woman who raised her, but never adopted her, Quantwilla says, "She's not a foster parent, she's a parent."[33]

Foster care *can* work.

A modern adoptive family

7
ADOPTION TOMORROW

No one could have predicted, a century ago, what adoption would be like today. No one today can predict what it will be like one hundred years from now—or twenty or even ten.

A CENTURY OF CHANGE

Only a century ago, adoption as we know it was virtually unheard of. In 1900, orphan asylums were still society's place of choice for homeless children. American children whose families were unable or unwilling to care for them were generally regarded as a source of cheap labor. Orphan trains, headed westward, were a second option. Few states had laws that recognized formal adoption.

Fifty years ago adoption was widespread, but its details remained cloaked in secrecy. Back then, adoption was for well-to-do white married couples and carefully matched healthy white newborns.

When lawmakers did begin writing adoption laws they drew them up based upon their deep-seated assumption that the only true families are those linked by blood ties. Even after adoption had become more commonplace, most people clung to the conviction that adoptive families were second-rate, less able than biological families to weather life's storms without breaking apart. In the interests of keeping adoptive families intact, legislators and social workers tried to make them seem as much as possible like "real" families. Birth parents were legally "dead" to the children they had given up. Adoptees and adoptive parents were matched according to rigid racial, ethnic, and religious criteria. Birth certificates were rewritten as legal fictions, creating the appearance of blood relationships that did not exist. In the end, the new adoptive family, intent upon keeping its "shameful" secrets such as infertility and illegitimacy to itself, pretended to all the world that it was no different from any other family.

It was a pretense impossible to maintain. Over the course of the twentieth century many men and women on every side of the adoption triad rebelled. Adoptees like Betty Jean Lifton fought for the right to know about their birth families. Birth mothers like Carol Schaefer spoke out about their pasts without shame and sought to find the children they had relinquished years before. Women working on adoption plans for their children began demanding open adoptions. They also wanted more of a say in deciding who their children's adoptive parents would be. Adoptive parents challenged the presumption that their families were somehow less stable than everyone else's.

In response, lawmakers and social workers gradually relaxed their rules and loosened their guidelines. Birth mothers were no longer treated as sinful "fallen women" who must be hidden away during their pregnancies and forced to surrender their babies at birth, sometimes without even seeing them. Birth fathers like Dan Schmidt were encouraged to assert their parental rights. The open-adoption movement grew and most states have legalized private and independent adoption as well. States and provinces established search registries, and adoption agencies began offering nonidentifying information to adoptees interested in learning about themselves. Oregon's Measure 58 became law.

But more change is needed. And today as in the past, it is those most intimately involved in adoption who will lead the way.

LEADING THE WAY

Dave Thomas, who was adopted at six weeks of age and grew up to found Wendy's Restaurants, is one of today's most visible adoption leaders. Among his goals: getting businesses that offer maternity or paternity leave—paid time off after the birth of a child, for example—to offer equivalent adoption benefits. "It's kind of a no-brainer," Thomas says of his contention that the adoption of a child is just as important to a family as the birth of one. "Today," he wrote in a column in April 2000, "about 62 percent of the Fortune 1000 companies [the thousand largest businesses in the United States] have adoption benefits, like paid time off and reimbursement for expenses like travel."[1] If Thomas has his way, that percentage will soon be 100.

Laura Blankman is less well-known, but still a leader. Blankman knows that society is more diverse today than ever before, a rich mix of race, religion, and national origin. That knowledge was part of what fueled her fight to adopt little Cornilous Pixley.

Joan Oleck is another leader. She's well aware that divorced and single parents are no longer the rare exception to the traditional two-parent household. In 1998, 27 percent of U.S. children were living in single-parent households. The vast majority of those households were headed by a woman.[2] If single women are allowed to have children, and raise children, why not allow them to adopt children? Keeping them from adopting is just one more way of implying that adoptive mothers are so naturally inferior to birth mothers that society must judge them by stricter standards.

Oleck sees her Manhattan neighbors Margaret and Camilla, the lesbian couple who adopted Miranda in China, as leaders, too. To Oleck, the threesome are proof that a family is defined not by who its members are, but by how those members live together. Miranda and her mothers do the same things that any loving family does. "We make breakfast," Camilla says. "We brush our teeth. We do laundry. . . . The thing we do different is teach our child about recognizing and embracing the fact that 'there are different kinds of families.'"[3] The

North American Council on Adoptable Children, which endorsed adoption by homosexuals who meet other standards for adoptive parenthood in 1998, has clearly learned something from successful parents like Margaret and Camilla.[4] Yet despite the group's endorsement, the right of homosexuals—and of single heterosexuals—to adopt remains uncertain today.

Some members of the adoption triad have moved adoption forward by finding innovative ways to solve adoption problems. In 1992, a birth father named Daniel Harriman and adopting parents Donna and Richard McDurfee found themselves locked in a legal battle like the one that had begun over Baby Jessica a year earlier. But the Baby Peter case had a very different outcome.

Peter, like Jessica, was born to a woman who was living with someone other than the father of her child at the time the baby arrived. Like Jessica's mother, Peter's mother lied about the father's identity on the child's birth certificate. Daniel Harriman learned about his son only after the McDurfees had started adoption proceedings based upon a plan worked out with the baby's mother. Harriman went to court to try to win custody.

He succeeded. But in a unique agreement with the McDurfees, Harriman and Donna McDurfee agreed to share custody of Peter. Peter would go on living with the McDurfees while Harriman retained visitation rights and continued to have a voice in the child's upbringing. The arrangement would be a little the way it would have been if Harriman and Donna McDurfee had been married and were now amicably divorced. As would happen after a divorce followed by a new marriage, Richard McDurfee would act as Peter's stepfather.[5]

Joy and Jim Jenkins are helping to lead the way in an entirely different area of adoption. In 1989 the Jenkinses became the first couple in the state of Arizona to adopt an infant suspected of having contracted AIDS from his birth mother. Up to then most social workers in Arizona and elsewhere assumed that AIDS babies were unadoptable, that no one would ever be willing to take in a child with even a remote chance of developing the syndrome. Although the Jenkinses were relieved that their son later tested negative for AIDS, they didn't stop there.

The two started a home-based project aimed at matching AIDS babies with preadoptive parents. Today the Children With AIDS Project of America lists over one thousand families waiting to adopt an AIDS infant. The project is supported by corporate sponsors and individual charitable contributions.[6] From "unadoptable" to a waiting list of over one thousand in a single decade is a remarkable change.

Could a similar type of project do anything to help reduce the enormous worldwide population of orphaned and abandoned children? Anthony D'Amato, the law professor from Northwestern University, thinks it might. He points out that already "international law has moved strongly toward saying that each child has a right to grow up in a family." Why not undertake an effort to turn that presumed right into reality?

"Private initiative and charity offer the best solution for bringing together children and adoptive parents," D'Amato says. The Jenkinses have proved him right on that point.

"The plan I propose might cost \$10 or \$20 million—a drop in the bucket for some major charitable foundations," D'Amato continues. "World centers, perhaps one per continent, could be set up where children and the people who wanted to adopt could be linked." Children would be brought to the centers by concerned adults: "lawyers, doctors, social workers, clergy." No money would change hands, so there would be little room for corruption. "People wanting to adopt would e-mail their names to an Internet site," D'Amato goes on. "After their suitability as parents was . . . established, their names would go on a waiting list." Adoptions would take place as children became available. Adoptive parents would be required to file yearly updates with regard to a child's health and education over the Internet.[7]

One appealing feature of D'Amato's plan, say supporters, is that it would allow social workers or others in an adopted child's home country to keep track of his or her well-being throughout childhood and adolescence. At the same time, it would enable the child and his or her adoptive family to maintain links with the land and people of his or her birth. A child could even stay in touch with members of his or her extended family—a sort of international open adoption. If enacted, the plan would make adoption less final, less irrevocable. In a way, it would mean combining some of the most positive elements of adoption with the advantages of kinship fostering as traditionally practiced in much of Africa and Oceania.

Tempering formally legalized Western-style adoption with some of the loving openness of kinship fostering would be a good idea all around, some adoption law experts believe. Elizabeth Bartholet, Harvard University law professor and mother of two adopted Peruvian children, is one of them. In other societies, Bartholet says, both biological and adoptive relationships are "far more fluid and flexible" than in Western European and American society. "My postadoption self wonders whether children in our society might not be better off if parenting relationships here were more qualified by choice and subject to change, with children encouraged to form a broader range of intimate connections and empowered to opt out of bad relationships," she writes.[8]

Pie-in-the-sky wishful thinking? Perhaps. But imagine how English Poor Law administrators of centuries past would have reacted to efforts like today's Children With AIDS Project. What would workhouse officials have made of Joan Oleck and Laura Blankman and all the other thousands of men and women who are doing so much right now to help children in need?

Today, adoption is for children and adults of all races, religions, and nationalities. It is for older children, foster children, and the disabled. It is helping to create all sorts of new, nontraditional families, and, slowly, it is helping those families win acceptance.

Adoption today is becoming a matter of pride and empowerment for adoptees and their families, biological and adoptive. These are hopeful signs for the future.

AFTERWORD:
THE ADOPTION PROCESS
IN A NUTSHELL

There are three main ways to arrange an adoption:

1. Through a private agency, licensed by the state and accredited by the Council on Accreditation for Children and Families Services. Many private agencies specialize in a particular type of adoption—international, open, and so on.

2. Through a public (state or county) agency. Public agencies commonly handle the cases of children already in foster care; often these include older and special-needs children.

3. Nonagency adoptions handled by a lawyer, facilitator, or the birth and adoptive parents them-

selves. Adoptive parents who initiate the process on their own often find prospects through newspaper ads, the Internet, or by consulting organizations.

All adoptions involve a formal relinquishment by the birth parent(s), a professionally conducted home study of the adoptive parents' residence, and a lawyer to help finalize the process.

STEPS IN THE ADOPTION PROCESS

1. Initiating the process. Both the birth and prospective adoptive parents learn how adoption works and how to locate each other.

2. Filling out an application form (in agency adoptions only).

3. Preparing a resume. The adoptive parents present an introductory letter, photos, and general background information for birth parents to review.

4. Arranging for a home study (adoptive parents only).

5. Training. Often public agencies require prospective parents to attend workshops over a period of weeks or months.

6. Waiting—anywhere from one to seven years in the case of a private adoption agency; less if the adoption is international, the agency is public, or no agency is involved.

7. Referral—a specific adoptable child is proposed to prospective adoptive parents. The latter can accept the referral or decide to wait for another child.

8. Establishing contact between birth and adoptive parents. Contact is most likely in private-agency and nonagency adoptions and least likely in the case of the adoption of a foster child. The contact may be onetime or ongoing.

9. Placing the child in his or her new home. Placement is followed by a waiting period, required in all states, before the adoption can become final.

10. Finalization—the legalization of the adoption in a court of law in the presence of a judge. The child's original birth certificate is sealed along with the court records of the adoption and a new, amended birth certificate listing the adoptive parents as the child's legal parents is issued.

11. Trained social workers offer birth and adoptive parents follow-up services (such as updating health records) after the adoption is final (in agency adoptions only).

SOURCE NOTES

CHAPTER ONE
1. Sullum, Jacob, "Adoption Pains," *Reason*, November 1999, p. 25.
2. "Adoption," *World Book Encyclopedia*.
3. Page, Susan, "Unprecedented Surge in Adoptions of Foster Kids," *USA Today*, September 24, 1999, p. 3A.
4. Pan, Esther with Sherry Keene-Osborn, "Culture by the Campfire," *Newsweek*, October 4, 1999, p. 75.
5. Lifton, Betty Jean, *Lost & Found: The Adoption Experience* (New York: The Dial Press, 1979), p. 14.
6. Branch, Jessica, "Do Adopted Children Have the Right to Know About Their Birth Parents?" *Glamour*, May 1999, p. 188.

CHAPTER TWO
1. Benet, Mary Kathleen, *The Politics of Adoption* (New York: The Free Press, 1976), pp. 23–4.
2. Benet, pp. 14, 29–31.
3. Benet, pp. 41–50.
4. Donovan, Aaron, "At Threshold of Old Age, Still Caring for Children," *The New York Times*, December 5, 1999, p. 45.
5. Grun, Bernard, *The Timetables of History* (The New Third Revised Edition) (New York: Simon & Schuster), p. 2.
6. "Old Testament," *The New Columbia Encyclopedia* (New York: Columbia University Press), 1975.
7. Genesis 15:1–4; 16:1–12; 17:16–17; 21:1–3; Benet, p. 25.
8. The Confederate Tribes 33: 1-5.
9. The Story 28:8–12; The Poets 26:11–22; Exodus 2:1–15; 3:1–10.
10. Benet, pp. 11, 38–9, 55–61.

CHAPTER THREE

1. Field, Rachel, *Calico Bush* (New York: The Macmillan Company, 1931), p. 9.
2. Hacsi, Timothy A., *Second Home: Orphan Asylums and Poor Families in America* (Cambridge: Harvard University Press, 1997), p. 16.
3. Forbes, Esther, *Johnny Tremain* (Boston: Houghton Mifflin Company, 1943), pp. 39–40.
4. Hacsi, p. 16.
5. Hacsi, pp. 12, 17, 22, 27.
6. Ashby, LeRoy, *Saving the Waifs: Reformers and Dependent Children, 1890–1917* (Philadelphia: Temple University Press, 1984), p. xi.
7. Hacsi, p. 20
8. Ashby, pp. 14, 20.
9. Hacsi, p. 34.
10. Webster, Jean, *Daddy-Long-Legs* (New York: Grosset & Dunlap, 1940), p. 43.
11. Ashby, p. xi.
12. Holt, Marilyn Irvin, *The Orphan Trains: Placing Out in America* (Lincoln: University of Nebraska Press, 1992), pp. 3–4.
13. Siegal, Nina, "Riders of 'Orphan Train' Meet to Tell Life Stories," *The New York Times*, May 13, 2000, p. B2.
14. Ashby, pp. 4, 7.
15. Hacsi, p. 44.
16. Benet, Mary Kathleen, *The Politics of Adoption* (New York: The Free Press, 1976), p. 66; "Adoption," *Encyclopaedia Britannica*.
17. Ashby, pp. 11, 31.
18. Benet, pp. 72, 120.
19. Jones, Cheryl, M.S.W., *The Adoption Sourcebook* (Los Angeles: Lowell House, 1998), p. 112.
20. Alexander-Roberts, Colleen, *The Legal Adoption Guide: Safely Navigating the System* (Dallas, TX: Taylor Publishing Company, 1996), p. 1.
21. Benet, p. 137.
22. Saffan, Sarah, "When the Search For Birth Parents Is a Search for Self," *The New York Times*, March 12, 2000, Section 2, p. 22.
23. Lifton, Betty Jean, *Lost & Found: The Adoption Experience* (New York: The Dial Press, 1979), p. 14.
24. Bartholet, Elizabeth, *Family Bonds: Adoption & the Politics of Parenting* (Boston: Houghton Mifflin Company, 1993), p. 48.
25. Lifton, Betty Jean, *Lost & Found*, pp. 3, 5, 21, 23, 27; Lifton, *Twice Born: Memoirs of an Adopted Daughter* (New York: St. Martin's Press, 1998), pp. 123–5.
26. Lifton, *Twice Born*.

CHAPTER FOUR

1. Lifton, Betty Jean, *Twice Born: Memoirs of an Adopted Daughter* (New York: St. Martin's Press, 1998), pp. 89, 98–9, 114.
2. Lifton, Betty Jean, *Lost & Found: The Adoption Experience* (New York: The Dial Press, 1979), pp. 73, 94, 127.
3. Lifton, *Twice Born*, pp. 125–7, 183, 235–40.
4. Verhovek, Sam Howe, "Debate on Adoptees' Rights Stirs Oregon," *The New York Times*, April 5, 2000, p. A1.
5. Jones, Mary Ann, *The Sealed Adoption Record Controversy* (New York: Research Center, Child Welfare League of America, Inc., 1976), pp. 1, 3, 6.
6. Jones, Cheryl, M.S.W., *The Adoption Sourcebook* (Los Angeles: Lowell House, 1998), pp. 117–9.
7. Rosen, Jennifer, "Found Her Family in the Funnies," *Good Housekeeping*, September, 1999, p. 28.
8. Lifton, Betty Jean, *Lost & Found*, pp. 101–2.
9. Brady, Lois Smith, "Peggy Cullen and Andy Matlow," *The New York Times*, October 3, 1999, Section 9, p. 9.
10. Herlihy, Kerry, "First Meeting," *Good Housekeeping*, December, 1999, p. 76.
11. "Ann Landers," *The Boston Globe*, December 22, 1999, p. F9.
12. Verhovek.
13. Lifton, *Twice Born*, p. 270.
14. Lifton, *Lost & Found*, pp. 20–1, 24.
15. Verhovek.
16. Branch, Jessica, "Do Adopted Children Have the Right to Know About Their Birth Parents?," *Glamour*, May 1999, p. 188.
17. Verhovek.
18. Beggs, Charles E., "Oregon Court Upholds Law Granting Adoptees Access to Birth Records," *The Boston Globe*, December 30, 1999, p. A12.
19. Leghorn, Theresa Kump, *The New York Times*, April 7, 2000, p. A22.
20. "Adoptive Parents Are Overwhelmingly in Favor of Opening Sealed Adoption Records, Cornell Study Finds," Cornell University News Service, Ithaca, January 30, 1997, press release.
21. Verhovek, Sam Howe, "Oregon Adoptees Granted Access to Birth Records," *The New York Times*, May 31, 2000, p. A16.
22. Wallace, Arthur, M.D., *The New York Times*, April 7, 2000, p. A22.
23. Alexander-Roberts, Colleen, *The Legal Adoption Guide: Safely Navigating the System* (Dallas, TX: Taylor Publishing Company, 1996), pp. 74–8; Jones, p. 142.

24. Foge, Leslie and Gail Mosconi, *The Third Choice: A Woman's Guide to Placing a Child for Adoption* (Berkeley: CA: Creative Arts Book Company, 1999), p. 112.
25. Thomas, Dave, with Constance L. Hays, "Success of a Happy Man," *The New York Times*, April 5, 2000, p. C10.
26. Alexander-Roberts, Colleen, *The Legal Adoption Guide: Safely Navigating the System* (Dallas, TX: Taylor Publishing Company, 1996), pp. 74–8.

CHAPTER FIVE
1. Garland, Nancy, "Wanted: Parents," *Bangor Daily News*, November 6–7, 1999, p. A1.
2. Benet, Mary Kathleen, *The Politics of Adoption* (New York: The Free Press, 1976), pp. 137, 140.
3. Hollingsworth, Leslie Doty, "Symbolic Interactionism, African American Families, and the Transracial Adoption Controversy," *Social Work*, September 1999, p. 443.
4. Meckler, Laura, "Adoptive Parents Looking Abroad," *Bangor Daily News*, November 27, 1999, p. D4.
5. "Adoption," *Encyclopedia Americana*.
6. Hollingsworth.
7. Garland.
8. Lee, Felicia R., "Bridging a Divide," *The New York Times*, April 30, 2000, Section 14, p. 1.
9. Hollingsworth.
10. Downey, Michael, "Canada's 'Genocide,'" *Maclean's*, April 26, 1999, p. 56.
11. Benet, p. 137.
12. Downey.
13. Alexander-Roberts, Colleen, *The Legal Adoption Guide: Safely Navigating the System* (Dallas, TX: Taylor Publishing Company, 1996), pp. 100–1.
14. Hollingsworth.
15. Bartholet, Elizabeth, *Family Bonds: Adoption & the Politics of Parenting* (Boston: Houghton Mifflin Company, 1993), p. 93.
16. Hollingsworth.
17. Brady, Lois Smith, "Aaron Gooday-Ervin, Toni-Ellen Weeden," *The New York Times*, July 23, 2000, Section 9, p. 7.
18. Meckler.
19. Oleck, Joan, "All you need is love–and a marriage license," Salon.com, July 9, 1999.
20. Hluchy, Patricia, "From the Great Wall, With love," *Maclean's*, May 10, 1999, p. 60.
21. Oleck.

22. Garland, Nancy, "Adopting New Attitudes," *Bangor Daily News*, November 27–8, 1999, p. A1.
23. Baker, Brenda, as told to Lynn Lovullo, "A Forever Family," *Parents*, June 1999, p.104.
24. Lee, Janice, "A Mother's Rescue Mission," *Good Housekeeping*, March 2000, p. 24.
25. Jay, Sarah, "When Children Adopted Abroad Come With Too Many Troubles," *The New York Times*, June 23, 1996, p. 1.
26. Lifton, Betty Jean, *Lost & Found: The Adoption Experience* (New York: The Dial Press, 1979), p. 52.
27. Bartholet, Elizabeth, *Family Bonds: Adoption & the Politics of Parenting* (Boston: Houghton Mifflin Company, 1993), pp. 91–2.
28. "Adoption," *Encylopaedia Britannica*.
29. Dewan, Shaila K., "Growing Up Asian, and Alone," *The New York Times*, July 26, 2000, p. B1.
30. Pan, Esther with Sherry Keene-Osborn, "Culture by the Campfire," *Newsweek*, October 4, 1999, p. 75.
31. National Adoption Information Clearinghouse, naic@calib.com., March 15, 1999.
32. Solot, Dorian, "Writing Lesbian, Gay, Bisexual and Transgender Homestudies for Special Needs Adoption," http://www.aresp.org.
33. Oleck.
34. Elliot, David, National Gay and Lesbian Task Force, delliot@ngltf.org, May 4, 2000.
35. Oleck.

CHAPTER SIX

1. Alexander-Roberts, Colleen, *The Legal Adoption Guide: Safely Navigating the System* (Dallas, TX: Taylor Publishing Company, 1996), pp. xiii, 134–9.
2. Many, Christine, "Baby Jessica Turns Nine," *Ladies' Home Journal*, February 2000, p. 17.
3. Alexander-Roberts, pp. 134–9.
4. "Woman, 27, Is Accused of Offering to Sell Child," *The New York Times*, April 3, 2000, p. B7.
5. Barry, Richard, "How Much Is That Baby on the Internet?," ZDNN, www.zdnet.com/zdnn.
6. Jones, Cheryl, M.S.W., *The Adoption Sourcebook* (Los Angeles: Lowell House, 1998), pp. 51–61.
7. Junnarkar, Sandeep, "Where Those Looking to Adopt Find Hope on the Net," *Cyber Times*, September 24, 1997.
8. Barry.

9. Oleck, Joan, "All You Need Is Love–and a Marriage License," Salon.com, July 9, 1999; "Wanted for Adoptions: Worldwide Standards," *Business Week*, June 14, 1999, p. 71.
10. Buettner, Russ, "Adopt 'Rip-Off' Hit," *New York Daily News*, September 13, 1996; Frankel, Mark, "One Year in Adoption Hell," *New York*, September 23, 1996, p. 40–45.
11. Oleck, "All You Need Is Love–and a Marriage License."
12. Jones.
13. D'Amato, Anthony, "Globalizing adoption," *Christian Century*, June 30–July 7, 1999, p. 668.
14. Oleck, "Wanted for Adoptions."
15. Altman, Lawrence K., "U.S. Issues Grim Report on the 11 Million Children Orphaned by AIDS," *The New York Times*, December 2, 1999, p. A12.
16. "The Invisible Children," *The New York Times*, February 20, 2000, Section 4, p. 12.
17. Baker, Brenda as told to Lynn Lovullo, "A Forever Family," *Parents*, June, 1999, p. 104.
18. Oleck, "Wanted for Adoptions."
19. D'Amato.
20. About.com>Parenting/Family>Adoption, May 20, 2000.
21. Sengupta, Somini, "Number of Foster Children in City At Lowest Level Since the 1980s," *The New York Times*, December 6, 1999, p. A1.
22. Schwartz, Robert, "Legal Delays Warp Children's Lives," *The New York Times*, April 29, 2000, p. A13.
23. Spake, Amanda, "Judges Push to Get Kids into Stable Homes," *U.S. News & World Report*, April 19, 1999, p. 62.
24. Page, Susan, "Unprecedented Surge in Adoptions of Foster Kids," *USA Today*, September 24, 1999, p. 3A.
25. Jones, pp. 61–2.
26. Spake.
27. Sengupta, "Number of Foster Children in City." Sengupta, Somini, "Hevesi Says Children Are in Foster Care Too Long," *The New York Times*, March 16, 2000, p. B2.
28. Yellin, Emily, "Group Seeks to Overhaul Foster Care in Tennessee," *The New York Times*, May 11, 2000, p. A27.
29. Sengupta, Somini, "Foster Care Agencies Fault Statewide Computer System," *The New York Times*, May 13, 2000, p. B3.
30. Sengupta, "Hevesi Says Children Are in Foster Care Too Long."
31. Bernstein, Nina, "When the Foster Care System Forgets Fathers," *The New York Times*, May 4, 2000, p. A1.

32. Sengupta, Somini, "Youths Leaving Foster Care System With Few Skills or Resources," *The New York Times*, April 28, 2000, p. A1.

CHAPTER SEVEN
1. Thomas, Dave, with Constance L. Hays, "Success of a Happy Man," *The New York Times*, April 5, 2000, p. C10.
2. *The World Almanac and Book of Facts* (Mahway, NJ: Primedia Reference, Inc., 2000).
3. Oleck, Joan, "All You Need Is Love–and a Marriage License," Salon.com, July 9, 1999.
4. Solot, Dorian, "Writing Lesbian, Gay, Bisexual and Transgender Homestudies for Special Needs Adoption," http://www.aresp.org.
5. Alexander-Roberts, Colleen, *The Legal Adoption Guide: Safely Navigating the System*, (Dallas, TX: Taylor Publishing Company, 1996), p. 138.
6. About.com>Parenting/Family>Adoption; Jimjenkins@aidskids.org.
7. D'Amato, Anthony, "Globalizing Adoption," *Christian Century*, June 30–July 7, 1999, p. 668.
8. Bartholet, Elizabeth, *Family Bonds: Adoption & the Politics of Parenting*, (Boston: Houghton Mifflin Company, 1993), p. 46.

FURTHER READING

Adamac, Chris. *The Complete Idiot's Guide to Adoption*. New York: Macmillan General Reference, 1999.

Brodzinsky, David M., and Marshall D. Schechter, and Robin Marantz Henig. *Being Adopted: The Lifelong Search for Self*. New York: Anchor Books/Doubleday, 1993.

Burlingham-Brown, Barbara M.S. *Why Didn't She Keep Me? Answers to the Question Every Adopted Child Asks. . . .* South Bend, IN: Diamond Communications, 1998.

Eldridge, Sherrie. *Twenty Things Adopted Kids Wish Their Adoptive Parents Knew*. New York: Dell Publishing Co., 1999.

Gabel, Susan, M.Ed. *Filling in the Blanks: A Guided Look at Growing Up Adopted*. Indianapolis, IN: Perspectives Press, 1988.

Krementz, Jill. *How It Feels to Be Adopted*. New York: Knopf, 1988.

Lifton, Betty Jean. *Twice Born*. New York: St. Martin's, 1998.

Lowry, Lois. *Find A Stranger, Say Goodbye*. Boston: Houghton Mifflin, 1978.

Paterson, Katherine. *The Great Gilly Hopkins*. New York: HarperCollins Children's Books, 1987.

Saffian, Sarah. *Ithaka: A Daughter's Memoir of Being Found*. New York: Dell Publishing Co., 1999.

INDEX